By George F. Kennan

The Cloud of Danger

GEORGE F. KENNAN

The Cloud of Danger

Current Realities
of American Foreign Policy

An Atlantic Monthly Press Book
Little, Brown and Company — Boston – Toronto

FIRST EDITION

T 08/77

LIBRARY OF CONGRESS CATALOG NO. 77-79616

ATLANTIC–LITTLE, BROWN BOOKS
ARE PUBLISHED BY
LITTLE, BROWN AND COMPANY
IN ASSOCIATION WITH
THE ATLANTIC MONTHLY PRESS

Designed by Susan Windheim

*Published simultaneously in Canada
by Little, Brown & Company (Canada) Limited*

PRINTED IN THE UNITED STATES OF AMERICA

To my wife, Annelise,
whose lack of enthusiasm for this and my other excursions into the realm of
public affairs has never detracted from the loyalty with which she supported
these endeavors.

Preface

On numerous occasions in recent years I have written articles or given speeches setting forth fragments of my thinking on different problems of American foreign policy, particularly our relations with the Soviet Union. Never have I attempted to pull together these various views and to distill out of them something resembling a grand design of American foreign policy. Increasingly, as time went by, the effort to do this came to appear to me as a duty I should not evade — should not evade, out of justice to my readers, who had a right to know how all these things fitted together, and out of justice to the thoughts themselves the value of which could not be measured before they had passed this comprehensive test.

The hard cold winter of 1977, coinciding as it did with the tentative, experimental phase in the activity of a new Washington administration, seemed a suitable time for such an exercise — and not only suitable but uniquely favorable. It was a time dominated by an intensive debate in American opinion over the question of how to deal with the Soviet Union. On the outcome of this debate there seemed to hang the entire future of American policy and of world events. This appeared to be a real and crucial parting of the ways: one road leading to a total militarization of policy and an ultimate showdown on the basis of armed strength, the other to an effort to break out of the straitjacket of military rivalry and to strike through to a more constructive and hopeful vision of America's future and the world's. Because this was so, and also for reasons of age, it seemed to me a case of "speak now or forever hold thy peace."

Various circumstances required that the book be written rapidly — in one breath, so to speak. There was no time for long research, for meticulous checking on accuracy of detail, for perfectionism in style and content. The book unavoidably assumed the form of what might be called musings on various of the questions treated; and the liberal use of the first person seemed unavoidable. Despite this informality, or perhaps because of it, the work may serve to outline one man's way of looking at the totality of America's principal problems and possibilities as an acting force on the world scene. If so, perhaps the casualness of presentation may be forgiven.

Contents

The Cloud of Danger

I

The United States as a Participant in World Affairs

ANY CONSIDERATION OF THE ROLE WHICH IT IS DESIRABLE FOR A country to play in international affairs, and of the purposes it might usefully pursue, has to begin with the nature of the country in question: of its needs with relation to its international environment, and the ways in which its internal constitution and habits affect its possibilities for action externally. Accordingly, before I approach the questions of this country's external involvements and commitments, I should like to remind the reader of certain internal conditions of American society which limit or complicate to a serious degree its freedom of action, or its ability to act effectively, on its external environment.

1. The Governmental Structure and Its Habits

It would be redundant to dwell at any length, here, on the congenital deficiencies of a government such as our own from the standpoint of the conduct of foreign policy. There is little to add, after the passage of nearly a century and a half, to what Tocqueville had to say on this subject in 1831. The sharp division of powers, which represented in the eyes of the founding fathers the very cornerstone of the American governmental system, already goes far to rule out the privacy, the flexibility, and the promptness and incisiveness of decision and action, which have marked the great imperial powers of the past and which are generally considered necessary to the conduct of an effective world policy by the rulers of a great state.

If there has been any change in this respect over the century and a half since Tocqueville wrote, it has been for the worse; because the American government of his day had at least the advantage of being a small government in a small society. The totality of its actions was never, at that time, hard to survey. The small number of persons then involved as actors on the governmental scene, executive, legislative and judicial, at least permitted easy and intimate communication among them, if it did not always promote agreement. Today, the United States government is vastly more complex and more diffuse. Its multitudinous involvements and activities defy comprehension by any single mind, not to mention control from any single center. If, therefore, the country was poorly fitted even in Tocqueville's day for a well-coordinated and purposeful participation in the hurly-burly of world politics, it is even less fitted, today.

Whether this situation has ever been adequately taken into account by the enthusiasts for American world leadership or imperial power is doubtful. The evidence of one great failure or folly of American statesmanship after another has seemed never to have been brought into association, in the minds of these people, with the way in which this country was constituted for the conduct of foreign policy in the first place. That we wandered into two world wars without adequate military preparation, and ended them without adequate political preparation, is a fact for which the statesmen of the respective periods are sometimes reproached, but almost never is the nature of our political system criticized. Nor does it seem to occur to us to ask whether the great miscalculations which led us into the folly of Vietnam were not something more than just the shortsight-edness of a few individuals — whether they did not in fact reflect a certain unfitness of the system as a whole for the conceiving and ex-ecuting of ambitious political-military ventures far from our own shores.

Be that as it may, one of the signal consequences of the Vietnam-Watergate experience was to cause, happily or unhappily, a further deterioration of our capabilities in this respect. For among those con-sequences we must note a serious diminution of such limited facili-ties for privacy as had previously existed within our foreign affairs establishment. In part, this is occurring through the extensive open-ing up of relatively recent archival materials to the scrutiny of press and public. But it is also occurring through the greater role that, by common consent, is now to be assigned to Congress generally in pol-icy formulation. President Carter has repeatedly expressed his inten-tion to consult extensively with the Congress, and to act in part-nership with it, in questions of foreign policy. And this only accords with a wave of publicly expressed sentiment in this direction, re-flecting the belief that one of the main causes of the misfortunes of the recent past lay in the high degree of executive secrecy behind which the respective policies and decisions were concealed.

Congress, then, is to be more extensively consulted and taken into confidence; and it is not my purpose to speak in opposition to such a state of affairs. It may all be for the best. But whoever talks about consulting Congress in major questions of foreign policy talks about forfeiting the advantages of privacy of decision, whatever these may be. This is no one's fault; it is simply inevitable, if only by virtue of the large numbers of people bound to be involved.

Nor is the loss of privacy the only way in which the process of policy formulation and execution will presumably be affected by the greater role that Congress is now to be allowed. No more than any other great legislative body can Congress act upon the conduct of foreign affairs by giving day-by-day discretionary guidance; it can act upon it only by establishing rigid norms, in the form either of laws or of treaties or of financial strictures, the effect of which is to bind executive action over long periods of time. Congress can, in other words, act upon foreign policy only fitfully, in great ponderous lurches which establish its direction, and the limits within which it can vary, for often prolonged periods into the future. This may well have a certain negative value, as an insurance against Executive folly; but it greatly limits, of course, flexibility of reaction on the part of the Executive, where it does not rule it out entirely. It makes it impossible for the Executive branch to react sensitively and effectively to changes in the objective situation that were not foreseen and could not have been foreseen (and the course of international affairs is replete with such changes) at the time when the respective congressional norm was laid down.

Congressional participation in the policy-making process, in short, not only reduces privacy of decision but inflicts upon that process a high degree of cumbersomeness and inflexibility; and these conditions, in combination, deprive the policy-maker of the possibility of initiative, the advantages of surprise, and the capacity for sensitive response to the unexpected.

Nor is this all. Congress is, unquestionably and inevitably, more vulnerable than is the Executive branch, and the State Department in particular, to pressures from ethnic and other organized lobbies or minorities, anxious to influence foreign policy to the advantage of their various parochial aims and concerns. The examples of this are so numerous that it would be superfluous, perhaps even invidious, to cite any single one of them. No one who thinks back over the annals of just these postwar decades will have difficulty bringing to mind a number of prominent instances in which ethnic minorities have brought pressures with a view to influencing foreign policy on behalf of what they perceive as the interests of their former mother country — interests which of course may or may not be identical with those of the United States. The industrial and union lobbies have done the same thing, and again on many occasions, in the selfish interests of minorities of the American citizenry — which interests, again, may or may not be identical with those of the country as a whole.

What has been most remarkable about these pressures has been not so much their existence, for they are in the nature of things, as the degree of their success. Example after example springs to mind of instances where they have proven more powerful and effective, as influences on congressional decisions in matters of foreign policy, than the views of highly competent persons in the Executive branch, who, in contrast to the lobbyists, had exclusively the national interests at heart.

When this sort of thing occurs, it simply means that the power of our government to act upon its international environment is being abused and distorted for domestic-political purposes, with the result that our actions on the external scene tend to become, as expressions of national policy, incoherent and either ineffective or self-defeating. And not only does this narrow the area in which the conduct of an effective policy is possible, but it provides an open incentive to foreign statesmen and their representatives to gain concessions from the United States not by a reasoned approach through the constituted channels of the President or the Secretary of State but by going through the back door and enlisting the support of particular American lobbies and persons in Congress whose purposes happen to coincide with their own. The examples of this sort of thing, too, have been numerous, including not only the activities of the China Lobby of the late 1940s and early 1950s but also the more recent alleged activities of South Korean agents in this country.

Now it may come as something of a surprise to the reader to be told that these comments on the congressional influence on foreign policy are not offered with a view to opposing the increased congressional role that now seems to be in the cards. I can well conceive that the way this country is now governed is substantially the only way a country of our size and extent *could* be governed, if one is to hold to democratic principles. It should come as no surprise to anyone to be reminded that there are always prices to be paid for democratic liberties. Perhaps this is one of those prices. If so, so be it. If the choice has to be made between a sacrifice of the blessings of democracy, on the one hand, or the achievement of a high degree of effectiveness in foreign affairs, on the other, I have no doubt where my own choice will lie.

But it is advisable for societies, as for individuals, to take realistic account of weaknesses they cannot control and handicaps they cannot overcome. My plea is only that if things are the way I have just suggested — if there is really going to be a heightened role of Congress in the foreign affairs process, with all that means in the way of the loss of privacy and flexibility and the enhanced influence of lobbies and other organized minorities on policy formulation — then the implications of this state of affairs for America's performance as a participant in world politics should be recognized, and the attendant lessons taken into account. Whoever insists on playing card games with all his cards face up on the table should avoid the fancier and more expensive game of poker. Whoever cannot help but signal to the outside world precisely how he is going to behave over long periods in advance, and binds himself to behave just that way and no other, should not entertain illusions as to the amount of day-by-day influence he is going to be able to exert on other governments; for the latter will long since have perceived, and made allowance for, the narrow limits of his freedom of action. And if, finally, a considerable portion of a government's behavior is to remain effectively outside the control of those charged with shaping its policy in the national interest, and is going to be determined on the basis of motivations and purposes not necessarily related to the national interest at all, then that government may as well recognize that it is destined to move through the forest of international events like a man with some sort of muscular affliction, obliging him to perform purposeless and self-defeating movements; and, recognizing this, that government will avoid getting into games which call for the utmost coordination and control of muscular power.

I see no reason to conclude that these various disadvantages are necessarily fateful from the standpoint of the security of this country. I do not see them as condemning us to any sort of helplessness or making it impossible to assure respect for our vital interests. But I can well conceive that they *might* have this effect if we should fail to take them into account and should try to conduct ourselves as though they did not exist at all. Because for societies, as for individuals, the beginning of wisdom, and not just of wisdom but also of the effective employment of one's own powers, is self-knowledge.

2. THE MILITARY-INDUSTRIAL COMPLEX

A second phenomenon of American life which has to be borne in mind when one thinks about this country's situation from the standpoint of the conduct of foreign affairs is the military-industrial complex. By this I mean, of course, the weight of military purchasing in our economy, the role of the Pentagon as a factor in our industrial life, and the effect of all this on our society.

The general outlines of this phenomenon are well known. Defense spending is now passing the one-hundred-billion-dollar mark, with the purchases of military hardware running well over $30 billion per annum, to which should be added, at least for purposes of this discussion, some $10 billion more for arms aid and sales to other countries.* This makes the Pentagon clearly the greatest purchaser in the United States, absorbing about 6 percent of the total national output of goods and services.

Now all this has several effects worth noting:

First of all, there is the inflationary effect. Whether the extensive purchasing of services and materials to be used for military purposes

* The involvement of the Pentagon with both military aid programs and arms sales to foreign governments is so extensive, and the effects of these programs are so similar to those of purchases for the U.S. forces, that they constitute an essential part of the problem here under discussion.

is or is not *in itself* inflationary is something about which economists, I gather, can and do disagree. (It certainly places in circulation enormous quantities of money in return for goods and services that are largely lost to the normal productive economy of the country.) But there could be no disagreement, I think, over the fact that it has strongly inflationary side-effects. No one who has had occasion to observe at first hand the workings of the armed services could fail to observe the lavish way in which money is used, as compared with functions that are obliged to meet the normal competition of private life. And it would be hard to believe that those who control military purchasing from the Pentagon end are generally able to exercise the same restraining pressure on the prices of what they buy as are private companies which have to meet the test of the balance sheet. Indeed, there are a number of reasons, including time pressures and the noncompetitive nature of many of the items purchased, why they would find it hard to do this even with the best of will and the sternest standards of integrity. (Having written this, I note the following passage from an article (*New York Times*, December 14, 1976) by Mr. Seymour Melman, Professor of Industrial Engineering at Columbia University:

Unlike civilian firms that traditionally minimize production costs to maximize profits, firms in the Pentagon's economy *maximize* all costs and the offsetting subsidies. These translate into rising prices.

The United States military economy is an inflation machine. From top to bottom cost and price increases are encouraged and rewarded; these practices are carried into and infect civilian parts of firms serving the Pentagon, and other enterprises. The classic processes of offsetting cost increases by mechanization and other efficiency-promoting measures are neglected. Higher costs are added to prices.)

Regardless of the extent to which the Pentagon may have been a contributor to the inflation, it has obviously been a major victim of it. The evidences of this are striking, and alarming. It is estimated that replacement costs of major items of equipment for the armed services, particularly aircraft and naval vessels, are now running three to five times higher than those of the items they are designed to replace, although many of the latter have been in use only a few years. The reduction in the size of various forces which was expected to take place, and to a limited extent did take place, with the termination of the Vietnam War, has not been attended by any corresponding reduction in military costs; on the contrary, it is now costing more, in a number of instances, to maintain the reduced forces than it did to maintain the larger ones of the pre-Vietnam and Vietnam periods.

All this testifies, in a general way, to the inflationary effects of great military spending; but it testifies also to a secondary fact of great importance, often missed in the discussion of problems of military competition with the Soviet Union: namely, that we are steadily pricing ourselves out of the running. Even if it were true that we were rapidly being overtaken and left at a disadvantage by the rate of development of the Russian armed forces (and about this I shall have something to say at a different point in this discussion), we ought to recognize that the reason for this, if carefully examined, would turn out to lie less in the pace and dimensions of the Soviet effort than in the wildly increasing expensiveness of our own. Considering the rate at which the costs of national defense are now being permitted to rise in this country, we can hardly expect to keep up in such a competition except at an enormous, steadily increasing, and finally almost prohibitive cost to our economy as a whole. Yet one sees little recognition of this in the public and congressional discussions of the defense budget. If the protagonists of heavy military spending really wished to find the shortest path to the correction of what they see as a growing disbalance to our disfavor in the relative strength of Soviet and American forces, they would do well to give more attention to our own inflation, and especially to the effects of that inflation on the military budget, and less to the effort to convince the rest of us of the menacing intentions and fearful strength of our Soviet opponents.

But there is another effect of the military-industrial complex, beyond the inflationary one, that deserves our notice. Such massive military spending leads to a curious double standard in the evaluation and use of money, as between those involved in this military spending and all the rest of us. It means that there is a group of people in Washington who, together with their counterparts in industry, are accustomed to thinking of millions of dollars in much the same way the rest of us think of thousands. One time, when I was at sea on one of our naval vessels and watching several forms of target practice, I was struck by the realization that each one of a certain class of missiles that were being fired off with great abandon (and not recovered) had cost more than my entire Pennsylvania farm, itself the product of generations of backbreaking work. Yet I am sure that this thought never entered the heads of the officers who were in charge of the target practice. And why should it? There were plenty more of these missiles where their stock had come from. No one asked about costs. No one had seriously asked about them when the missiles were originally ordered. In the view of those who did the purchasing, these costs were chicken feed.

Now I am not saying that this sort of thing could be avoided. The activities of the military in peacetime consist, after all, of playing with a great many expensive toys; and it is hard to find criteria of financial prudence applicable to the process of playing with toys. But I *am* saying that it leads, unavoidably, to a double standard in the way people think about money. And this double standard makes it hard to find valid means of comparison between military needs and those of the civilian economy. When military spending grows to such vast dimensions, and proceeds at such vast and inflated expense, it tends to cut loose from all normal considerations of relative usefulness as compared with other functions of our governmental and economic life and to begin to lead a life of its own in a never-never world where three zeros are added, as though it were the most natural thing in the world, to every normal figure, where millions become for their manipulators what thousands are to the rest of us.

It becomes a question, then, how the billion-dollar economy is to be controlled, indeed whether it can be controlled at all, by those whose concepts are formed in a whole different stratum of monetary values.

To this we must add the reflection that this vast flow of military spending comes to constitute a vested interest on the part of all those who participate in it and benefit from it. This includes not just the industrialists who get the money, and the Pentagon purchasers who get the hardware and services, but also all those who benefit from the arrangement in other ways: not only the uniformed personnel of the armed services but those who serve the Pentagon directly as civilian workers, and beyond them the many more who, as workers in defense plants or in other capacities, share in the spin-off from these vast expenditures. These latter alone are estimated to number over two million. All of these people come, of course, to have a stake in the perpetuation of high defense spending. And since the workers in defense industry, in particular, tend to live in compact blocs in single congressional districts, and to be associated with powerful unions, their political punch is powerful. The individual congressman finds himself exposed to pressures from three sides: from the industrialists, who want the orders and the money; from the military, who want the hardware and the services; and from the defense workers and their unions, who want the defense-connected jobs. This is a powerful combination — so powerful, in fact, that it sometimes compels the congressman himself to become in effect a shareholder in the huge vested interest which it all represents.

What this means is that our practice (now a habit) of permitting the Pentagon to put out more than a hundred billion dollars each year for what are ostensibly the requirements of national defense has become something much more than a feature of defense policy — it has become a species of national-economic addiction — a habit which we could not easily or rapidly break, in fact, in the course of anything less than several years, even if the entire external justification for it were to disappear — even if the Soviet Union were to sink tomorrow, with all its armies and missiles, to the bottom of the ocean.

I am not trying to say, here, that there is not, along with these internal compulsions, a serious measure of justification for such expenditures arising from the real needs of national defense. But I am saying that these two motivations coexist in the governmental decisions out of which our defense expenditures flow, and that it is very difficult to decide, in any given instance, where one stops and the other begins. Defense spending, in other words, is not just a means to a single end: the assurance of our external security in an uncertain and unstable world; it is also a condition of American society — one which has profound effects on our domestic-political life, and one which constitutes one more limitation on our ability to shape and execute our foreign policies in response to external challenges.

For the designing of one's defense posture — the measures one takes, that is, in the development of armed strength — are not just domestic measures: they are, whether one intends them this way or not, acts of foreign policy. They affect other governments. They influence the policies those other governments pursue. Yet here, in the field of defense preparation and defense spending, we have a set of acts of foreign policy the dimensions and nature of which we cannot determine just on the basis of external necessity alone. To an appreciable extent we are obliged to perform certain actions in this field on the basis of domestic-political necessity, carry us where they will in our external relations. And this is only another way of saying that we are faced here, once again, with a limitation on our freedom to conduct a foreign policy which would be, from the standpoint of its external effects, coherent and consistently purposeful.

3. THE ENERGY DEPENDENCE

In a series of public lectures delivered in 1954 at Princeton University, the writer of these lines, concerned over the implications of the bestowal of the status of complete sovereignty on an increasing number of small or underdeveloped political entities, made the following observations which he hoped (in vain) would become the subject of some national discussion:

. . . we have . . . largely conceded the right of any other sovereign government to do anything it wishes with regard to the raw material resources on its own territory, even though this may mean the invalidation of existing foreign contracts and the abrupt disruption of arrangement for the sale and distribution of such materials to other countries. The fact that other countries may have become extensively dependent on these arrangements is not . . . considered to be any proper formal grounds for insistence on respect for their interests. Against such things as capriciousness and irresponsibility on the part of the government of the raw-material exporting countries, or the sudden denial of raw materials as a means of political extortion, there is apparently no theoretical recourse. . . .

Pointing out that a number of sources of raw materials important, and in some instances essential, to the stability of our national economy were situated on the territories of new states, to whose governments we could not realistically look for great maturity and sense of responsibility in the handling of their external affairs, I went ahead to say that for this reason,

in many instances our raw material supply hangs on slender threads, and ones over which we have no power of control or even of redress. And I worry lest some day drastic interruptions of this supply should lead to painful crises and tensions. . . . I wonder whether it would not be the part of kindness and liberality, in reality, to face up to this problem today by making it plain to other governments that they must not permit our great and . . . delicate economy to become dependent on them in this way unless they are prepared to acknowledge a clear obligation to guard the durability and reliability of the respective arrangements.*

In uttering this warning, I had in mind not only oil but also other strategic or economically vital minerals. In the case of the minerals

* *Realities of American Foreign Policy* (Princeton: Princeton University Press, 1954).

my anxieties would seem to have been exaggerated. With the partial exception of bauxite, cobalt, and manganese, where an abrupt denial by foreign suppliers could create short-term difficulty and possibly force us to resort to more expensive substitutes, there is little prospect that we could be put under serious pressure by action of the supplier-nations. But in the case of oil, these fears proved justified to the hilt. In 1973 our country did indeed find itself faced with just such a "drastic interruption of . . . supply," as I had anticipated: in the form of the Arab oil embargo of the end of that year. And the sharpness of this challenge was multiplied by the fantastic 400 percent boosting of the prices for petroleum products that accompanied it.

Actions of this nature could, as we have just seen, have been foreseen. What could not have been foreseen was the incredible failure of response on the American side. Instead of taking account of the lesson implicit in the embargo and proceeding at once to reduce its dependence on Arab oil, the United States government permitted the American oil companies to resume purchases from the former boycotting countries, and then permitted our dependence on foreign oil to grow, over the ensuing years, from 24 to 42 percent of our consumption, and our dependence on the Arab producers, in particular, from 11 to 18 percent.

One stands stupefied at the frivolity and irresponsibility reflected in this response — or lack of response — to a challenge of the utmost gravity — a challenge not just to the economic interests but to the political independence of this country. The extent to which American society is today dependent on the supply of oil for support of its economic life needs no emphasis. A sudden diminution even of anything in the order of 18 to 20 percent of the regular supply (and it is this which the Arabs now have it in their power to inflict) could wreak havoc not just with the existing transportation system of the country but with a thousand other facets of our economic life, including agriculture. Never, since the days when coal was the lifeline of all industrialized societies, and possibly not even then, has a great nation had a more vitally sensitive economic artery, and one by the damage of which it could more easily be paralyzed, than has the United States of 1977 in the flow of oil as a source of energy for a great portion of its economy. To permit our society to become helplessly and abjectly dependent on foreign rulers, generally, for the continuance of a major portion of that flow was in itself a major and inexplicable failure of statesmanship. But to permit such a dependence to endure, and to increase, with relation to a group of rulers with whom we have political differences of the most serious nature, and ones that cut directly into one of the most sensitive points of our domestic-political life — namely, our relation to the political future of the state of Israel: this simply defies comprehension. One cannot envy the future historian who will someday find himself compelled to seek a plausible explanation of such complacency.

We hear it said that it was right for us not to react firmly to the Arab boycott of 1973–1974, and right not to take measures to reduce our dependence on Arab oil in the ensuing period, because to have done so might have been to offend the more moderate of the producer-governments involved and thus to have forfeited the benefits of such limited political collaboration as they might otherwise have been inclined to extend. Such a position, implying as it does that we have already accepted our state of inferiority — that we are now obliged to approach the supplier-governments only as supplicants and to consider ourselves grateful for such crumbs of consideration as may from time to time fall from their table — is a shameful one for a great power to adopt. It may have its short-term benefits; but its long-term effect can only be the perpetuation of the forfeiture of respect — for our qualities as a nation and for our vital interests — which we have already incurred.

The situation just described would be bad enough if its negative effects were confined to the direct impact on our energy supply. Unfortunately, those negative effects, as everyone knows, carry much further and are felt by the world at large. The aggravation of world-inflationary tendencies; the heightened strain on the finances and economies of developing countries; the resulting jeopardizing of the soundness of the massive indebtedness of those developing countries to the more developed ones; the accumulation in the hands of the rulers of the oil-producing countries of vast quantities of money, far beyond their capacity to spend to any good effect; the stimulation of a highly unhealthy level of arms purchasing by certain of those governments; the accumulation in Western banking establishments of unsound levels of short-term deposits representing portions of this excess capital: in the face of all these phenomena, too, the United States has shown itself incapable of any reaction beyond a pained and helpless wringing of the hands.

It would still be possible, though much more difficult than it would have been three years ago, to devise and carry through a program designed to rid the United States of this dependence, at least to such a degree as to restore to us a bargaining power not inferior to that of the producing countries themselves. No single measure would suffice to this purpose, but a combination of measures might. These would have to include a serious effort at energy conservation, adequate stockpiling of oil, and a determined effort of research and development looking to the uncovering of alternative sources of energy.

But such a program, even if we were politically prepared to embark upon it, would take time — more time than it would have taken if it had been put in hand three years ago, when it should have been. Meanwhile, the capacity of this country to play an effective part in world affairs, and particularly in the crucial area of the Middle East, will continue to be partially lamed by its enduring energy dependence. This, too, has to be borne in mind when one addresses oneself to the problems of what are normally viewed as "foreign affairs."

4. THE DEVELOPING DOMESTIC PRIORITIES

The phenomena to which I have just pointed — the congenital handicaps, the military-industrial complex, and the dependence on foreign oil — are ones that affect directly this country's ability to conduct a purposeful and effective diplomacy. There is one more factor which has to be included in this listing, although its effect is less direct. This is the growing priority which, as I see it, is going to have to be accorded to domestic concerns, to the detriment of external ones, in the coming years.

I do not wish to labor this point, but I must explain what I mean by it. There are a whole series of negative phenomena in American life which, if allowed to continue and to become worse, will eventually become intolerable and will call, then, for drastic, painful and expensive solutions.

We have a great and serious problem in the disintegration of certain of our great cities, and outstandingly the greatest of them, New York — a problem which is not just a physical and social one but has the most serious sort of implications for the health of cultural life across the nation. The country as a whole has a stake in the vitality of its greatest cultural center, and cannot permit that vitality to be destroyed without suffering the consequences in a hundred ways. As of today, we are not mastering that problem. We have not yet even taken the true measure of its causes.

We have an appalling problem of violent crime in large parts of the country. This, too, we are not mastering. We have shown ourselves unable to achieve even the first step in the mastering of it, which would be a ban on the open sale and legal possession of firearms. Unwilling to take even this first step, we are unlikely to proceed at any early date to the even more rigorous ones that the depth of the problem demands.

We have a problem of inflation which we have not only failed to master but have in effect given up hope of mastering, because it would involve the imposing of an inconvenient degree of discipline on both business and labor.

We have a problem of unemployment which we have similarly failed to master, largely because to attempt to do so would mean to question the soundness of the existing minimum wage, to come into conflict with the unions, to make people accept jobs they don't want to accept and in places where they would prefer not to have them, and to shoulder the burden of developing various possibilities for part-time employment and self-employment and obliging people to avail themselves of them before going on the relief rolls.

We have a chaotic and disgracefully inadequate system of public passenger transportation, not to mention facilities for the movement of mail and parcels. We are the only great country, indeed the only advanced country, without a decent telegraph system. Our efforts to improve these conditions, weakened by our incurable conviction that such functions should properly be viewed as commercial ones, have been feeble, confused, and unconvincing.

Instead of developing public transportation and creating effective incentives to its use we continue to permit our society to be over-whelmingly dependent on the private automobile, surely the most wasteful, antisocial, and environmentally pernicious means of moving human bodies about that has ever been devised. We have permitted our dependence on this contraption to grow, like the military-industrial complex but in a much more serious way, into the quality of a national addiction, a habit — more than a habit, in fact: a way of life — from which we could not suddenly emancipate ourselves without withdrawal symptoms of the most appalling sort. Someday, if only because of the growing scarcity and expensiveness of energy, we will have to break away from this addiction; and it is none too soon to begin, as the Arab oil embargo should have taught us. Yet no serious effort in this direction has yet been made; and we continue to rejoice every time we read in the papers that the market for cars — and large cars — has improved, because, as we see it, this means increased employment for the automobile workers. Who cares, then, if new hordes of machines are poured out to choke already crowded streets and highways?

We have a problem of declining educational standards, at least in a very large segment of our educational establishment. The causes of this are obviously multiple; but, such as they are, we will not face up to them, because to do so would be to fly in the face of the prevailing passion for "democratization" in the educational process and of the widespread conviction that the schools ought properly to serve primarily social goals, and only secondarily educational ones.

There are other problems, primarily of a cultural nature, which I am inclined to include in this list, although I do so with some hesitation, because I know that to few others will they appear as important as they do to me. Among these would be such things as the corruption of the process of mass communication by its abandonment to the mercies of the advertisers — an evil which debauches, and drains of educational value, a system of television which is probably no less important than the entire formal educational system as a force for the shaping of the outlooks, the values, and the intellectual habits of our people. I would also like to include what seems to me to be the absurdity of the strike as a means of settling labor differences in functions where the safety and convenience of the general public is at stake. Someday, we shall have to come away from this primitive device, which bears the same relationship to social justice as did the mediaeval "trial by battle" to individual justice in earlier ages. Meanwhile, it hampers progress in a host of ways.

Particularly would I like to include the shameful phenomenon of the wildfire spread of pornography not only along the streets of our cities but on the screens and pages of our media of communication. This is a form of decadence in the face of which we, including unfortunately even our courts of law, have shown ourselves, once again, uncertain and helpless. Only a confident and inborn sense of good taste could have suggested the proper line beyond which normal freedom of expression ends and the commercial exploitation of salacious curiosity begins. Lacking this sense of taste (as it would appear), we fumble along, ineffectively, in a forest of legalisms.

Finally, I must mention the serious inadequacy of the American press and electronic media from the standpoint of informing and instructing the American public in matters of foreign policy. A whole series of their attributes: not only the predominance of advertising, as mentioned above, among the concerns of their proprietors, but also the hasty, disjointed, and staccato nature of most of their offerings; the low educational level of the great majority of the reporters and announcers; the persistent tendency to overdramatization; the fascination with the trivial at the expense of the essential; the overcoverage of the peregrinations and utterances of senior figures and undercoverage of the deeper trends of international life — all these reduce the ability of these media to serve as an effective force for educating public opinion in the field at hand. There is not a daily newspaper in the country that compares, from the standpoint of foreign news coverage, with the great papers of Western Europe, such as *Le Monde* and the *Neue Zürcher Zeitung*, and there are only three or four that even approach them. This general failure must explain such phenomena as, for example, the positively weird misconceptions about Russia and "communism" that prevail in large parts of the western sections of this country.

I shall mention one more phenomenon of our domestic life which probably exceeds all these others as a future claim on our attention and resources, at the expense of foreign policy, and about the importance of which there can be much less argument and disagreement: and this is the continuing problem of environmental deterioration. Here, unquestionably, there is already a vigorous reaction. Awareness has grown. Measures have been and are being taken. But it would be wildly optimistic to say that we have yet even approached the point where we would be gaining on this problem. In a number of areas, deterioration is proceeding apace. Soils are being eroded. Fine arable soil is continuing to slip away into the hands of the developers and thus to be lost to agriculture — and this in an age of increasing famine in great areas of the earth. Wetlands, so essential to Nature's balance and to the salutoriness of environment generally, are still being allowed to succumb, regularly, to the developer's bulldozer. Inroads continue to be made, for mining and grazing purposes, on our national parks and wilderness areas. Forests continue to fall victim to the inexhaustible appetite of the advertising media for wood pulp. Water tables continue to fall in many parts of the country, in the face of a general complacency. We have scarcely touched the problem of pesticides; these and other poisonous chemical wastes are still finding their way, as is human sewage, into our streams and lakes, and through them to the world oceans. We have discovered, in fact, no fully satisfactory way of disposing of human wastes, not to mention the much more serious problem of the nuclear ones. The construction of nuclear plants is proceeding apace, even in the absence of any satisfactory answers to the attendant problems of waste disposal and thermal pollution.

What is most serious, with respect to this environmental problem, is the growing evidence that the total cost of coming to grips with it, social and financial, will be much greater than was originally supposed. As our experience turns from the warnings of the environmentalists to actual efforts of public authority to stop pollution it becomes more and more evident that the real culprit here is not just the *abuse*, from the environmental standpoint, of the processes of industrialization and urbanization but those very phenomena themselves: that the problem cannot be mastered, in other words, without reversing to some extent both of those processes. Environmental considerations are apparently going to demand, if the proper relationship between Man and Nature is to be restored to this country, a partial reversal of trends of development which for decades have lain at the very heart of the American idea of progress. The relationship of city to country — of urban life to rural — is going to have to be altered, to some extent, in favor of the latter. Highly complex and refined processes of industrial production are going to have to be abandoned, in some instances, in favor of more primitive ones which involve less, not more, division of labor. Processes that are expensive in terms of input of materials are going to have to be abandoned in favor of ones that are more costly in terms of input of labor. Some things now done by machine will have to be done by handicrafts methods. There will have to be more part-time jobs: fewer hours put in at the factory and more at the backyard vegetable garden and orchard. Nature's free offerings will have to be more widely tapped, through small windmills and dams and sun reflectors, to relieve the strain on the power lines. There will not have to be anything resembling a total abandonment of this highly complex modern system of life and production by which we now live; but it seems increasingly doubtful that what needs to be accomplished in the way of environmental adjustment can be done just by tinkering with it, alone. A certain sacrifice in substance, in the form of a return to simpler and more labor-intensive modes of life and production, will apparently be necessary.

If this analysis is correct, then the strains this problem is going to impose on our society in the coming years are going to be severe beyond anything heretofore contemplated. Unless there is an unforeseen development in automotive transportation people will have to learn to live closer — within walking or bicycling distance — to the facilities on which their lives depend; they will not be able to depend on the automobile to get them, at any time, anywhere within 30 to 40 miles of their home. This, however little people like it, is bound to take a higher level of planning and directing by public authority. This is foreign to both American experience and American tradition; and the acceptance of it will not occur without much tension and agony. But this is what faces us in the final years of this century; for if the deterioration continues, it will finally assume forms so painful that adjustments of the sort just mentioned, far-reaching and unpleasant as they may appear, will become more and more acceptable by comparison with the alternatives.

These phenomena are mentioned in this context because coming to grips with them will necessitate a diversion of both attention and resources from foreign policy to domestic concerns. We will not, in other words, be able simultaneously to be all that we have tried, since the recent war, to be to others and all that the developing situation will require us to be to ourselves.

On the success or failure of our efforts to come to grips with these various problems depends much of our force and persuasiveness in world affairs. If we are to be something more to other peoples than just an intimidating military power, we will have to concern ourselves with the image of our society that is projected to the rest of the world. There is not one of the phenomena listed above that does not affect this image — sometimes in very important ways. One of the first requirements of clear thinking about our part in world affairs is the recognition that we cannot be more to others than we are to ourselves — that we cannot be a source of hope and inspiration to others against a background of resigned failure and deterioration of life here at home.

5. Conclusions

Of the four factors I have mentioned as limitations, present or future, on our freedom of action as a participant in world affairs, the first — the way in which our government is constituted for the conduct of foreign policy — is so far, not just from correction, but even from recognition as a serious problem, that any thought of changing it within the foreseeable future may as well be dismissed. It was my hope that the Bicentennial would be an occasion for reviewing the political institutions of this country, as they have developed over the course of the years, with a view to seeing whether they could not be improved in the light of the challenges with which we are now faced. Nothing of this sort, however, was done. Re-enactments in costume of such events as the Battles of Lexington or Princeton seemed to commend themselves to public authority as a more suitable way of marking the anniversary. If such a review was not conducted at this point, it will scarcely be conducted for many years to come.

In the other three instances, however, the steps that are required are not, in theory at least, beyond the capacity of public authority as it is now constituted; and one may hope that in some areas, if not in all, further progress will be made.

I would like to point out, however, that in all three instances — in taking the military-industrial complex under control, in overcoming our dependence on the Arabs and other OPEC countries for our supply of oil, and in mastering those various problems which, if not soon mastered, are going to produce something resembling a profound crisis of our national life — the steps that need to be taken are ones that would normally be thought of purely as measures of domestic affairs. Yet, as I have tried to show, they are ones that affect most intimately our posture, and our capabilities, as a world power. And therein lies a lesson which many people in our country have been slow to learn: namely, that foreign policy, like a great many other things, begins at home — that the first requirement of a successful foreign policy is that one places oneself in a favorable posture for its conduct. This means, of course, designing and shaping one's society consciously to this end. And this in turn means bearing in mind, as one approaches domestic problems, the effect on foreign affairs of those decisions one has to make.

II

The Global Scene

GIVEN THE KIND OF COUNTRY WE SEEM TO BE AND THE LIMITATIONS that rest upon us as participants in world affairs, let us look at the outside world and see what challenges, what dangers, and what opportunities for usefulness it presents. And let us take first, if only to dispose of certain questions that are sometimes raised about the global aspects of our foreign policies, those features of our international environment that have, or are often viewed as having, important global implications.

There are very few of these. I can think, in fact, of only four that deserve mention here. One is the form of organization of international society that has come into existence, and acceptance, at this stage in history. A second, about which we hear much talk, is the advancing food shortage in large parts of the world. The third is the question of humanity's progressive destruction of its own natural environment, insofar as this problem presents itself in global terms. The last is the question of the weight we should give, in designing our policies, to their possible effects on the form of government prevailing elsewhere in the world.

1. THE ORGANIZATION OF INTERNATIONAL SOCIETY

At the end of the last century, the society of nations was organized for the most part on what might be called hierarchical lines, in the sense that there was a differentiation, at least in part hierarchical, in the way various political entities related formally to one another. First, there was the small group of "great powers" (five or six was the accepted figure in the nineteenth century). These were surrounded by a group of smaller but well-established independent states. The difference between the two categories was recognized in formal diplomatic practice, the great powers being represented in one another's capitals by ambassadors, whereas only "ministers" were exchanged with, and among, the others.

Beyond this category of clearly independent and sovereign states, and usually but not always subordinate to one or another of them, there was a wide spectrum of minor political entities: vice-royalties, protectorates, colonies, residencies, principalities, sheikdoms, caliphates, other autonomous or largely autonomous entities of one sort or another. Some of these participated in international life only through the medium of the greater power to which they were subordinate. Others participated in part that way, in part independently. Still others participated, insofar as they did so at all, independently, but in reduced degree, involving themselves only in those international questions in which they had a direct interest.

This order of international society, with its hazy distinctions, many of which would today be considered invidious, lacked uniformity and often covered relationships that were onerous or obsolescent. But it had the advantage of permitting some allowance to be made for the wide variety and instability of the political arrangements under which various peoples find it possible to live in this world. It allowed flexible adjustment to the changing degrees of advancement and of the capacity for contributing to international life by which societies were marked. It was also capable of making allowance for geographic limitations: for tiny political entities that had

[28]

become the traditional forms of political cohesion on remote islands or in mountain valleys. The very multiplicity, and, if you will, the very fuzziness, of the various categories of status which this order of international life provided, allowed for an accommodation to real cultural and physical differences which a more rigorous order of international society would have found it difficult to effect.

Today, all this has changed. Beginning in part before World War II but then, overwhelmingly, in the postwar period, it seems to have been agreed that any group of people, regardless of how small, how backward, or how poorly constituted to make any useful contribution to international life, which professed a wish to have conferred upon it the status of sovereign independence, should have its wish recognized (except where this group had the misfortune to be included in one of the great Communist states, or one of the newer African ones, in which case it was generally conceded that the rule would not apply). The result has been, as everyone knows, that the number of entities to which has been conceded, by common consent of the members of the international community, the right to call themselves sovereign and independent has grown from the original 50 who constituted the founding members of the United Nations to something on the order of 160, of which some 147 (it is hard to keep up) are now members of that organization.

In this way, a single status — that of nominal independence and unlimited sovereignty — has become the garb in which the overwhelming majority of the political entities of this world appear on the international scene — indeed, the only garb in which they *could* appear, since scarcely any other is recognized. Under this single description one finds entities composed of hundreds of millions of persons, occupying huge segments of the fertile and productive areas of the world's surface; but one also finds, under the same heading, tiny communities, in some instances hardly more than a village and its surroundings, whose interest in world problems is as insignificant as their capacity for rendering any appreciable contribution to the solution of them. All of them — the monster countries and the tiny

[29]

ones — enjoy, theoretically, the same status, with the same rights, privileges and duties, including voting rights in the UN General Assembly. An absurdity? Yes, you may say, but a harmless one. I am not so sure that it is harmless.

Aside from bloating the various diplomatic corps across the world, this reckless squandering of the recognized status of unlimited sovereignty and independence has watered down the meaning of those very concepts. It has made a mockery of the fundamental principles of international organization, and has greatly reduced the usefulness of international entities — notably those of the UN and its associated agencies — which were set up to perform important and potentially constructive purposes. This prodigal scattering of the status of sovereign independence has led to the establishment, within a number of those UN bodies (UNESCO, the ILO, and the World Health Organization are examples, but the outstanding one is of course the UN Assembly itself) of majorities, the irresponsibility and emotional instability of which is such that the potential value of the organizations in question has been seriously reduced. The practice, in other words, has proved destructive of much of what might otherwise have been the capacity of international organization for alleviating world problems. It has constituted a destructive abuse of the value of universal international organization per se.

The damage is now done. There is no possibility of undoing it. A modicum of usefulness remains to the UN, particularly in functional fields where activities take place directly under the authority of the Secretariat; and this must be preserved to the extent possible. But the United States is obliged to recognize that as a result of this folly (in which it participated very prominently and for which it bears a high measure of the blame), the possibilities for achieving useful improvements in world conditions through global international organization have been grievously reduced. Much of what, in other circumstances, might have been done that way will now have to be done either by unilateral or bilateral action or by agreement among smaller, more serious and more responsible groups of governments.

Meanwhile, Americans might do well to take stock of the conceptual errors that led them to contribute so generously to this debauching of the meaning of sovereignty and the potential values of international organization. There were two such errors, intimately connected. One was the notion that "democracy," a term applicable in reality only to the relationships of individuals to the governmental power in a body politic, is also applicable to the interrelations of governments in an international society — the belief, that is, that in an international body governments can suitably be given the franchise, by analogy to the position of individuals in a free society, on the principle of "one government — one vote." This is a complete misconception, particularly insofar as it ignores the artificiality of the criteria by which an authority is classified as a government, as well as the wildly disparate qualities that mark entities bearing that name.

The second of the conceptual errors underlying the American contribution to the present unrealistic and ineffective order of international society was the curious liberal-American assumption that bigness on the part of a political entity is somehow bad, smallness good: that large powers are by nature wicked, small powers innocent and virtuous. Resting on this assumption was the vision, so agreeable to American sensibilities, of the United States defying the recalcitrance of the established powers and principalities of this world and sweeping to world leadership at the head of a following of grateful and admiring smaller states. This childish daydream, the roots of which run back well into the last century, has affected American statesmanship on more than one occasion; and there can be no question of its connection with the enthusiasm with which we watched, and abetted, the conferring of the status of sovereign independence on a horde of wholly untried and inexperienced small entities, in whose responsible conduct as full-fledged members of the world community we had not the faintest reason for confidence.

The damage, I repeat, is now done. It is not soon to be repaired. It will eventually have to yield, some way or other, to the realities of international life. But we would do well to take account of the true sources of this failure of statesmanship on our part, lest they trip us up again in future contingencies — and in even more serious ways.

2. THE IMPENDING FOOD-POPULATION CRISIS

Another problem that is often discussed and viewed in global terms is that presented by the virtual certainty of large-scale famine in several parts of the world in the remaining years of this century. The fact that this problem is so often considered as global is in itself the reflection of a serious misconception; for the problem is not really a global one — it is primarily regional. The effort to depict it as a global one rests on the assumption that it is a situation that ought properly to engage the conscience of all mankind, and particularly the rich United States. The impression is often conveyed that it is a condition which we, in our abundance, could cure if we wished to — if, that is, we were less selfish and more self-sacrificing.

My only purpose here is to point out that none of this is correct. We in the United States did not create this problem (it is fundamentally an unavoidable result of overpopulation), and it is far beyond our powers to solve it. Such surpluses as we are capable of producing out of our own agricultural effort would scarcely scratch the surface of the difficulty, even if we were to do all in our power to increase a surplus and to decrease our share in the consumption of it. This is not a question of the will. This is a question of statistical fact.

I seem to recall that many years ago, when I was serving in the Department of State, an American vice consul in one of the provinces of India wrote a highly factual report, amply supported by seemingly unchallengeable statistics, proving that the entire annual American grain surplus of that day could be added to the food supply of this one Indian province, and yet, divided as it would have had to be among some eighty million people, it would still not raise the calorie intake to a level consistent with normal standards of adequate nutrition. The Department of State received the report, as I recall it, with shocked embarrassment, and exerted itself neither to call wide attention to it nor to ponder its lesson, for it ran counter to the prevailing philosophy of the time. But the lesson it suggested is still applicable, and on a far greater scale.

The above is not meant to suggest that we should do nothing at all in response to this situation. We may well continue to do what little we can through the multilateral organizations that concern themselves with the problem. More important still, we might find means to moderate our self-indulgent and wasteful habits in the use of food: placing narrower limits on the amount of grain that is fed to animals and then consumed in the form of animal products, and increasing the proportion consumed as cereal food, which represents a much more economic use of it. This will not appreciably help those nations that face the prospect of famine-by-overpopulation in this coming period; but it will put us in a better posture with relation to the problem as a whole. This is not the last occasion we shall have to note that the cosmetic aspects of our behavior are also ones that deserve attention. If one cannot oneself cure certain unfortunate world conditions, one can at least contrive to look as though one cared.

But this, note well, is again, like so many of the things that need to be done to improve our world position, in the first instance a matter of domestic rather than foreign policy. Until we learn that domestic-political convenience must not always be regarded as supreme — that it must occasionally defer to the demands of a suitable role and posture of this country in world affairs — a large number of our problems of foreign policy will continue to be unmet.

3. THE ENVIRONMENTAL PROBLEM

Mention has already been made of the environmental problem as it imposes itself upon the domestic policy-maker. But this is a problem that also has its international aspects, fully commensurate in importance for Americans and their lives with what they do, with relation to the environment, at home.

Some years ago, on the eve of the first great international gathering devoted to international environmental problems — the Stockholm Conference of 1972 — the writer of these lines published in *Foreign Affairs* an article intended as a contribution to the thinking about the problems which the forthcoming conference evoked. In it he named certain principles which, he thought, would have to underlie any effective international action in this field. He opposed, in the first place, coupling or confusing environmental problems with the problems of economic development. He opposed, for various reasons, assigning to the United Nations the responsibility of leadership in the development of international action designed to halt environmental deterioration. He thought it better that this work be taken in hand by a group of the leading industrial and maritime nations — the nations which created the most serious aspects of pollution, which had the resources to study the problem, and which had it in their power to remedy most of the evils in question. He saw nothing to be gained by involving Third World countries, most of which had little interest in environmental problems and even less ability to do anything very useful about them, in this field of activity. He further thought that what was needed was not just an agency which would be powerless to act except on the basis of a new international consensus on each question, and could then act only through the respective governments themselves, but rather an international environmental *authority* which would have, in certain fields (and notably in the great international media of the high seas, the Arctic and Antarctic, the stratosphere, etc.), its own power of decision and enforcement. And he thought, finally, that the sponsoring and supervising

[34]

agencies of this authority, and the source of its personnel, should be not the various governments, acting directly, but such of the major scientific bodies of their respective countries as each of them might designate, so that the scientific community would be charged, in effect, with the conduct of the entire operation, the governments confining their role to that of selecting the scientific organizations which were to participate, providing the financing, and giving other forms of support.

The Stockholm Conference came and went; and in not one respect did these views, if they were ever considered, find acceptance. The upshot of its deliberations was that environmental considerations should indeed be extensively coupled with developmental ones — the very deliberations and decisions of the conference seemed, in fact, to be dominated by the Third World countries. Leadership of the subsequent action was indeed entrusted to the United Nations. Instead of the leading industrial and maritime nations being charged with carrying the action forward, a body was set up by the United Nations (the Governing Council for Environmental Programs), consisting of the representatives of fifty-eight governments under an executive director to be elected by the General Assembly of the United Nations, and with a headquarters to be established in Nairobi. The great scientific bodies of the major powers were to have no direct part in this operation. Among the fifty-eight participating governments, those of the Third World turned out, not unexpectedly, to have a clear majority.

I do not mean to belittle the achievements of the Governing Council. I have no doubt that, directed as it has been by an able and dedicated man (Maurice F. Stone), it has made the most of the narrow possibilities allowed to it by the form in which it was established. But it is obvious that the treatment of environmental considerations was subordinated, at Stockholm, to developmental considerations, and the subsequent arrangements and activities have continued to reflect this subordination.

It is not surprising, in the light of these facts, that the progress made in recent years has been something less than spectacular. Particularly is this true of the problem of the pollution and other misuse of the high seas. There is still no proper enforcement agency for such international agreements as exist concerning pollution of the seas by oil. The construction and operation of monster tankers goes on apace, although no one can be unaware of the dangers they present from the standpoint of possible maritime pollution. Nothing has been done about flags of convenience; and hundreds of vessels continue to be operated on the high seas with no adequate regulation from the standpoint of safety — safety to themselves and to the coasts near which they operate. As these words are being written, we are suffering the eighth serious accident (two of them being major disasters) in American territorial waters by flag-of-convenience vessels within a space of some two weeks. Surely the time has come to take measures (and both domestic and international ones are needed) to put an end to this shocking abuse of the privilege of operating vessels on the high seas.

The erection of oil rigs in international waters is wholly out of hand. There is no one who can speak for the ocean and its inhabitants in the face of massive pollution of it from rivers and seaside communities. There is no one to gainsay, with any degree of authority, the people, including the seaside communities of the American East Coast, who want to dump noxious or poisonous wastes into international waters. There is no one to decide whether it is or is not safe for nuclear-powered vessels to ply the seas. There is, in short, no one who can exercise on the high seas the sort of control individual governments now exert within the steadily expanding zones which they claim as their territorial waters. There are people who speak for governments; there are none who speak for the ocean and its inhabitants.

The part played by the United States government and its representatives in this phase of international life during recent years has of course embraced a multitude of facets; and only a long labor of research could support a sound critical assessment of it in its entirety. Suffice it to note, here, that there is, so far as I am aware, no evidence that Washington has exerted itself very seriously at any point to avert the trend of events described above. Here, again, a wholly new level of imagination and determination would be in order if the United States were to accept, and exert, the leadership in this field which its status as the world's greatest industrial nation, and the world's greatest single pollutor, would seem to demand of it. A good beginning would be a re-examination of the principles on which international action has proceeded, or not proceeded, since the Stockholm Conference, with a view to seeing whether a more hopeful and effective approach might not still be found to this world problem, the seriousness of which is increasing by the day.

4. THE "THIRD WORLD" AND THE NORTH-SOUTH DIALOGUE

The "Third World" is a vague and highly variegated concept. This means that anyone undertaking to discuss America's relationship to it in general terms is wandering out onto treacherous ice. Obviously, to anything he may say, there will be abundant exceptions. Nevertheless, there are a few observations I feel moved to make.

One is struck, on reading most of what is written about "North-South" relations and noting what is said in international bodies on this subject, by the constantly recurring suggestion, or inference, that the advanced industrial countries, and outstandingly the United States, are in some way at fault for the disparity between their degree of development and that of the countries of the Third World — that this is the product of some sort of injustice inflicted by them on the Third World countries — and that they are in duty bound to repair the injustice by doing all in their power, even to the point of sharing their wealth and diminishing their own prosperity, to remove the disparity and to bring to the Third World peoples a level of development and prosperity similar to their own. Otherwise, we are allowed to suppose, things will be very bad: the peoples of the Third World, tired of this injustice and unwilling to wait longer for its removal, will rise in their wrath — and where will the advanced countries be, then? The responsibility for removing this disparity, finally, is seen to lie overwhelmingly on the side of the governments and peoples of the advanced countries. It is up to them to determine whether, as one American journalist (writing from South Africa) recently put it, "the white-dominated technological world will come to terms with decolonized regions known as the 'Third World.' "

Historically seen, the whole vast process of development of relations between the more advanced countries of Europe and North America and the less developed peoples in the southern continents was clearly in many respects a tragic one; and I have no desire to ignore or dispute the fact that many — sometimes even great — mistakes were made from the European–North American side. Nevertheless, I do not see these mistakes as a general cause of the present relatively low degree of development in Third World countries; and I cannot overcome a sense of bewilderment in the face of the view that sees in this disparity the expression of some sort of general wickedness or moral failure on the part of the "white-dominated technological world."

I have before me, as I write, a faded snapshot, recently sent to me by a relative, of the log house in which my great-grandparents lived when they first came, in 1851, to the Green Bay region of Wisconsin: a crude, almost windowless structure, standing in a dreary treeless field. And I am moved to recall that the Wisconsin of that day was very much what we today would call an undeveloped country.

Well, these people worked hard, as did most of those who came after them. They were the bearers of a now spurned and ridiculed "work ethic" (which was not only a Protestant one). They were, for the most part, also the bearers of a long tradition of local self-government; and they contrived, as did people in other frontier states, to set up and operate governmental institutions, based on habits of tolerance and respect for majority opinion, which spared them the wastage of internecine violence. Wisconsin prospered, therefore, under their ministrations, and is today the seat of a high prosperity — too high, I sometimes think, for the good of its own inhabitants. All this was done, be it noted, without any form of external assistance other than the normal investment of out-of-state capital, some American, some foreign, on which the Wisconsinites were expected to pay the usual return in interest and profit or forgo further such assistance.

Now is there, I ask myself, something morally wrong about this — with relation to peoples elsewhere, and particularly to the similarly underdeveloped ones of other continents? Had we Wisconsinities been a lazy, violent, improvident people, devoted more to war than to industry — had we wasted what little substance we had on civil strife of one sort or another, or had we been for other reasons unsuccessful — and had we therefore remained undeveloped instead of developing our resources — would we today be seen as the possessors of a peculiar virtue vis-à-vis the more developed countries, entitling us to put claims on their beneficence and to demand of them that they exert themselves to promote our development? Would they then have been guilty before us for their greater success? And is no credit whatsoever to be given in this modern world for the old-fashioned American virtues of thrift, honesty, tolerance, civic discipline, and hard work? These, after all, were the qualities that permitted Wisconsin to become "developed" in the course of a century. The climate, as every Wisconsinite knows, did not particularly conduce to that end.

Unless someone can suggest to me other answers to these questions than I have found to date, I must maintain that the first thing we need to do in our approach to the Third World is to divest ourselves of our guilt complex and our self-consciousness generally with relation to it, and learn to look representatives of the countries of that great region firmly in the eye when we deal with it.

The second thing we have to do is to bear in mind that what we can or could do to help the Third World is very little in comparison with its developmental needs. Development has to come, in overwhelming degree, from within, not from without. Even if this were not true, the scale of the requirements far surpasses our resources.

What we *could* do is twofold. First we could, theoretically, get ourselves partially out of the line of fire by abandoning those several aspects of protectionism that handicap the developing countries in their efforts to export to the United States. Secondly, we could put more money into their hands through the international organizations that occupy themselves with aid to backward countries.

The first of these options we are unlikely to use, because American foreign policy normally operates, as we have seen, only within the area in which it encounters no serious resistance from powerful American lobbies or pressure groups; in this instance such resistance would have to be expected, in abundance.

The second would not do much good, actually, because of the general limitations that rest on the ability of outside parties to bring development to countries that suffer under severe internal handicaps; but it would put us in a better posture and would be moderately beneficial from the standpoint of public relations.

This said, it is hard to see what the problem is, and why, in particular, there should be so much talk of some sort of North-South "dialogue" or, failing that, "confrontation." Beyond what has just been mentioned there is really little the United States, in particular, can do for the Third World. And there is equally little the Third World, with the exception of the OPEC countries (who don't need aid), can do to vent its frustration on the United States or the other highly industrialized countries. In the long run, the countries of those continents will have to work their passage, as did our own forefathers, or the passage will not be made. Meanwhile, both parties, the advanced industrial countries and the underdeveloped ones, may as well stop the empty talk of grand agreements between North and South, and apply themselves, each of them, to their own tasks.

That the United States will continue for the moment, in these circumstances, to be the target of much verbal abuse, cannot be doubted. But this bombardment must be expected to diminish in the degree that the United States shows itself indifferent to it. For much of it was invited by the very self-flagellation on the part of earnest Americans to which it supplies the echo. An America less self-accusatory would be the object of less accusation — from this quarter, at least.

5. "Democracy" as a World Cause

We continue to hear it said or suggested in a thousand ways and from a thousand sources that a major concern of American diplomacy, worldwide, should be the advancement of self-government by other peoples. Our government is criticized for allegedly supporting Latin American "dictators." It is criticized for failing to support (as the critics see it) "majority rule" in Southern Africa. It is urged to make the repressive actions of the Soviet government towards dissident intellectuals an issue in Soviet-American relations. In a host of ways the thought finds expression in the American media that America has a duty to encourage and support the growth of democratic institutions, or at least the assurance of human rights, across the world, and that this should constitute a major, and even over-riding objective of American policy on a global scale.

There are a number of reflections which cause me, for one, to have deep misgivings about this thesis.

First of all, I know of no evidence that "democracy," or what we picture to ourselves under that word, is the natural state of most of mankind. It seems rather to be a form of government (and a difficult one, with many drawbacks, at that) which evolved in the eighteenth and nineteenth centuries in northwestern Europe, primarily among those countries that border on the English Channel and the North

Sea (but with a certain extension into Central Europe), and which was then carried into other parts of the world, including North America, where peoples from that northwestern European area appeared as original settlers, or as colonialists, and had laid down the prevailing patterns of civil government. Democracy has, in other words, a relatively narrow base both in time and in space; and the evidence has yet to be produced that it is the natural form of rule for peoples outside those narrow perimeters.

All distinctions in forms of political authority, including that which people try to draw between "democracy" and "dictatorship," are of course relative, not absolute. There is a bit of conspiracy, and of authoritarianism, in every democracy; and a bit of democracy in every dictatorship. Besides, people influence each other. Political fashions and pretenses have a way of spreading. The urge to play at being "democratic," in the sense of setting up institutions the names of which suggest self-government, has affected most of the world. Few governments fail to support some pretense of this nature; even the names they often choose for themselves ("People's," "Democratic," "Republic," etc.) are designed to convey this suggestion. Possibly, this has some significance for the future. It seems to have very little for the present. Some of the nastiest and most brutal tyrannies now masquerade under titles of this nature. Even if "democracy" were the wave of the future (and the longer span of history affords no grounds for supposing that it is), the future in question would not be the immediate one; and whoever made it his objective to realize the dream of a democratically governed world in any short space of time, to the sacrifice of more pressing needs of the international community, would be behaving very quixotically indeed.

Secondly, I know of no reason to suppose that the attempt to develop and employ democratic institutions would necessarily be the best course for many of these peoples. The record of attempts of this nature has not been all that good. Time and time again, authoritarian regimes have been able to introduce reforms and to improve the lot of masses of people, where more diffuse forms of political authority had failed. As examples one has only to think of Portugal under Salazar, of China under Mao, even of Cuba under Castro, because, distasteful as the Castro regime may be to many people (myself, I may say, included), we have to accept the testimony of dispassionate witnesses that it has introduced many useful reforms and done much for the common people. If the question be asked whether the great popular masses of this world, as distinct from restless intellectuals, prefer democratic institutions to prosperity and economic security, it would be a brave man who would undertake to answer that affirmatively in the light of the historical record. Those Americans who profess to know with such certainty what other people want and what is good for them in the way of political institutions would do well to ask themselves whether they are not actually attempting to impose their own values, traditions, and habits of thought on peoples for whom these things have no validity and no usefulness.

Finally, I think we should note that if America were to try to become, as John Quincy Adams put it disapprovingly, the "guarantors" instead of the "friends" of the liberties of half the world, there is no reason to suppose that we would make a very good job of it. One notes that even among those Americans who profess the most passionate attachment to this cause, the actual application of the enthusiasm is highly selective. They seem, in fact — these advocates of efforts to assure the liberties of other peoples — to fall into two categories: those (the Greeks, the Jews, the Cubans, the blacks, etc.) whose interest is largely confined to the political fortunes of people of their own ethnic origin; and those others, the professional liberals, whose concern for the cause of democracy elsewhere purports to rest on general principles but seems to confine itself in actuality to the brutalities of right-wing authoritarianism, as in Chile or Greece, or to those of white European authoritarianism wherever the latter affects people of different racial identity. These preoccupations lead to heavy pressures on the United States government to intercede on behalf of Jewish dissidents in Russia, of Castro's opponents in Cuba, of Chilean oppositionists, and of various African resistance leaders striving for the removal of white power in Southern Africa in favor of the establishment of their own. They show no comparable concern for the nameless and numberless Chinese who may have fallen victim to the rigid intellectual and physical discipline of the Chinese Communist regime; for the several tens of thousands of Africans slaughtered just in the course of recent years by other black Africans who had the power to slaughter them; for the Indians abruptly and brutally expelled from Kenya and Uganda; for the thousands of Angolan blacks forced to flee across the border into Southwest Africa and to seek the protection of the South African authorities; nor indeed, in the case of the Soviet Union, for the hundreds of thousands of non-Jewish people (Crimean Tartars, Volga Germans, and what you will) who are still suffering from the measures taken against them in the Stalin period. These and other such peoples simply do not fit into the highly selective limits to which the enthusiasm of various Americans for other people's liberties is normally confined.

There is every reason to suppose, therefore, that even if the United States government were to accept a solemn commitment to devote itself to the cause of the promotion of democracy in other parts of the world, the ensuing measures of policy would not be apt to reflect any very fair and principled devotion to this cause. What would be more likely to happen would be that the commitment would be instantaneously seized upon by factions within the American citizenry interested in achieving certain objectives relating to those who were their particular *bêtes noires* among other governing groups or those who were the particular objects of their sympathy among those out of power. The other victims, or subjects, of authoritarianism — those who had no constituency among the members of these American pressure groups — would continue to be ignored, as they are today.

Nor is there any reason for confidence that the results of such

American efforts to interfere in the internal affairs of other countries would invariably lead to any great improvement in the respective governmental conditions, even if the efforts in question were nominally successful in achieving the overthrow of the regimes against which they were directed. There is a tendency among Americans to assume that anyone who finds himself victimized by, or in opposition to, a given dictatorship or authoritarian regime is ipso facto a fighter for freedom, devoted to the principles of liberal democracy, and certain, if helped to political success, to adopt these principles and to carry them into practice. American diplomatic history affords one example after another of this naïve assumption. Things are, unfortunately, seldom just this simple. Too often, the highest hope of political dissidents in an authoritarian society is the dream of someday treating their tormentors as their tormentors have treated them — an objective not likely to have anything to do with the principles of democracy. By and large, successive governments in a given society tend to resemble each other in methodology if not in professed ideology. Particularly in a society accustomed to brutal or authoritarian rule, it is hard for anyone to govern, however lofty his original intentions, by methods strikingly different from those to which people have become accustomed by long experience and traditon.

For all these reasons it is difficult to see any promise in an American policy which sets out to correct and improve the political habits of large parts of the world's population. Misgovernment, in the sense of the rise to power of the most determined, decisive, and often brutal natures, has been the common condition of most of mankind for centuries and millennia in the past. It is going to remain that condition for long into the future, no matter how valiantly Americans insist on tilting against the windmills. American policy-makers would do better to concentrate on those areas of international relations where the dangers and challenges are greatest and where America has the greatest possibilities for useful and effective action. These, as it happens, are ones that have little relation to the cause of democracy as such. And they are quite enough to absorb all the energies and resources we can devote to them.

6. SUMMIT DIPLOMACY

I have just spoken about several *problems* commonly regarded as global ones. There is, in addition, one practice of the United States government so widely employed as to be considered as global; and it too deserves a word of comment.

Meetings of heads of state and senior statesmen in multilateral gatherings occurred occasionally in the century preceding World War I, but they were not frequent, and they were used, as a rule, only to mark great occasions. The immediate aftermath of the First World War produced a certain increase in the frequency of such gatherings, often under the aegis of the League of Nations; but it was only in the years following World War II that the practice multiplied many times and began to overshadow normal bilateral diplomatic contacts as forums for the transaction of international business. It was embraced with particular enthusiasm by a number of American statesmen. So luxuriously has the practice grown that it would be tedious to attempt to recount the foreign travels of American statesmen just in the past decade. Things have now gone so far that the failure of a senior American statesman — President or Secretary of State — to appear at certain fairly frequent and regular multilateral gatherings of this sort assumes the quality of some sort of negative political gesture.

Precisely because this has now become so widely accepted a practice, it would obviously not be practicable to try to abandon it entirely and abruptly at the present time. Nevertheless, every effort should be made to reduce the number and frequency of such travels and attendances by presidents, secretaries of state, and other officials of cabinet level.

The reasons for this are several.

First of all, such occasions, especially if they occur far away from Washington, are wearing, time-consuming, and distracting for the statesmen concerned. This is true notwithstanding the speed of airplane travel; indeed, if the flight crosses several time zones, it involves the added strain of jet lag. And the actual proceedings of such meetings, particularly if they involve formal speeches and much translation, generally require a good deal of wasted, or nearly wasted time, not to mention the numerous ceremonial and protocolaire interruptions. The encounters thus represent an added, and for the most part unnecessary, burden on the energies of a man already normally burdened to the limits of his strength by the regular duties of office.

Secondly, while the statesman in question is sitting in these high-level meetings, or in his airplane going and coming, he is not at his desk, and is not giving normal day-to-day attention to the hundreds of other areas of American foreign policy which ought to be receiving that attention. His absence is always felt at his office at home; and there is a tendency for things to slow up, for action and decision to be delayed, while awaiting his return.

Thirdly, when a President or Secretary of State occupies himself personally with a single problem of foreign policy, or with a small circle of problems, such as normally constitutes the agenda of a summit meeting, it tends to paralyze attention to that problem at lower levels in the Department of State for long periods after his return. People tend to say: "Oh, that's something the President [or the Secretary of State] is handling personally," and to shy away from taking any initiative or responsibility in the handling of it themselves. The personal involvement of the senior official in communicating with a foreign government in places far removed from Washington interrupts, in other words, the normal rhythm of the work of the State Department.

Fourthly, when one of the highest American officials comes to a foreign country and deals directly with his opposite number there, it affects unfavorably the position of the regular diplomatic representative at the post in question. He is obliged, in the times between summit meetings, to function as the personal representative of the President. For this he needs all the prestige he can be given. The sudden self-insertion of President or Secretary of State into the matters he has normally been handling tends to set him back and to diminish his value in the eyes of the foreign government. In earlier years, it was regarded as obligatory that the ambassador should be present at any meeting between his President or Secretary and their foreign opposite numbers of the country to which he was accredited. Now, not even this is always observed. Often the summit-level negotiations take place in Washington, while the ambassador is left at his post. All this means that he is often not even properly informed of what has been done, and is obliged to try to find it out by such gossip as he can eke out of the local government. This, again, diminishes his prestige, and with it his usefulness to his own government in the periods between summit meetings.

Next, the Chief of State, or the busy Secretary of State, is often — for several reasons — not the best person to conduct detailed negotiations with a foreign government. He does not have the expertise of the regular representative. He is usually too busy to master all the details of the subject at issue, and seldom contrives to read the bulky briefing books prepared for his edification. The very seniority of his position leads to expectations that he will make decisions and commitments on the spot, whereas the necessity, under which the lower-ranking representative finds himself, of reporting back to Washington at each stage of the negotiation, gives ample time for reflection and study. The senior figure, furthermore, cannot, when handling something personally, be easily disavowed if he makes a mistake. There is no cushion of higher authority to absorb either such mistakes as he may make, or such asperities as may arise, during the negotiations.

Nor is this all. When persons of supreme or high authority deal directly with one another, there is a tendency for their agreements to take on a personal quality and to depend for their validity, to some extent, on the personal relationship that has been established. This is sometimes fine as long as it lasts; but the agreement is then largely vitiated if one or the other of them falls from office. Agreements concluded through the regular diplomatic channels, time-consuming and cumbersome as this may be, and thus regarded as agreements between governments rather than between individuals, tend to be more carefully worked out, less personally conditioned, and more enduring.

Lastly, the presence and antics of large bodies of pressmen at the meetings of senior figures present a real hazard from the standpoint of the effective conduct of intergovernmental business. The reporters and photographers make privacy of decision far more difficult than it would otherwise be. Their presence and their efforts encourage leaks. They overdramatize for the public whatever they are able to learn, raise unwarranted expectations, and impede a proper public understanding of what is done.

Never are they as happy as when they contrive to discover and to inflate any residual differences or minor conflicts and stumbling blocks that may occur in the negotiating process. The regular diplomatic representative, going about his mundane daily business, generally escapes these treacherous attentions; for the press and the media are interested only in the episodic: they have little patience for the steady humdrum of diplomatic representation and intercourse in which so much of the world's business, and often the most useful part, is performed.

One can only hope, therefore, that the new American statesmen, their predecessors having had more than their fling at the histrionics of summit diplomacy, will now be concerned to wean themselves from this enticing but pernicious form of conducting foreign policy, and will at least have a try at the practice of staying at their desks and applying themselves daily, as so many of the rest of us are obliged to do, to the tasks for which they were elected or appointed. They might be surprised at the results.

7. WORLD ECONOMIC PROBLEMS

I am making no effort in this discussion to treat of world economic problems and the obligations and opportunities that the United States might have with relation to them. Problems of this nature are esoteric, vastly complex, and highly unstable. Their contours change with bewildering speed. They involve private interests more importantly than the actions of government. And I am not at all sure that they can be usefully treated at all, insofar as governments have to treat them, on a global basis; I suspect that one has to be much more specific, more pragmatic, more national, or at best more regional, in approach.

There is a great deal of talk, these days, about interdependence. To what extent this interdependence really exists and constitutes a commanding reality of our time, I cannot say. I will only say that however much there is of it, as a feature of the situation of the United States, I wish there were less. It is all right as a component of our relationship with the great trading nations, such as Japan and the countries of Western Europe. Beyond that, overinvolvement with others economically begins to become a danger, both because the others are so widely capable of letting us down, and because we, too, if pressed by certain domestic hardships and necessities, are quite capable of letting *them* down.

If we are to play a useful part in guiding the great adjustments that have to be made within our own country and internationally with a view to achieving a safer situation for ourselves and others, we will require a reasonably large measure of control over the flow and the usage of our own resources. This we will not have if we become too extensively involved with others. The dependence on foreign oil is an example of this.

Let us not be carried away, therefore, by a passion for foreign trade and for external economic and financial involvement. Within limits, these things have their economic uses. Carried too far, they become limitations on one's own freedom of action, and sometimes — what is even worse — unnecessary vulnerabilities, hampering, if not paralyzing, independent action.

8. CONCLUSIONS

The general upshot of these reflections, if they may be said to have one, is that America's possibilities for usefulness, as an active partner in world affairs, do not lie on the global plane. Neither is the international community organized in a manner as would conduce to effective action through international organization on a global scale, nor are those particular areas of world affairs which commend themselves to many Americans as suitable ones for a global approach ones in which much can be actually achieved on this basis. The world is too vast, too complex, geographically and historically too differentiated, to lend itself to such sweeping and grandiose approaches. We will get farther, in the search for constructive and hopeful possibilities in American statesmanship, if we turn, as we shall now do, to individual regions, countries and problems.

III

Latin America

FEW OF THE READERS OF THIS BOOK WILL NEED TO BE REMINDED THAT I am no expert on Latin America. I have not even been there for over a quarter of a century. Nevertheless, when I think about American foreign policy I am obliged to consider that part of the world, along with the others. In all of this, I resemble a great many other American citizens who also have not recently been there!

I thought, in visiting that part of the world in 1950, that I could detect a certain tragic quality in its civilization: the product of a combination of factors, including the less happy accidents of geography, the enduring trauma of the cultural shock once administered to the Indian populations by the Spanish conquest, the rigidities of the Spanish cultural and political tradition, and so on. But beyond this I was, and am, well aware of the danger of generalization in thinking about so vast and varied a region and about the problems it presents for American policy-makers. I know that no two of its countries are alike, and no two of its statesmen. Like other great regions of the world, it is better dealt with in its specifics than in generalities.

For this reason I shall avoid speculation on the problems presented by our relations with Central and South America as a whole (some of them will come up in other contexts) and confine myself, at this point, to the two questions that seem to be, at the moment, most critical and urgent in the demands they raise for American policymakers.

1. THE PANAMA CANAL

It is now three years that the question of the future of the American relationship to the Panama Canal has been preempting much of the time of Latin American gatherings and a good deal of the headline space of American newspapers. The reason is, of course, that Panama, with the unanimous support of the remainder of the Latin American community, has been vehemently demanding the abandonment of the 1903 treaty, on which the American position at the Canal Zone has rested for so many years, and its replacement by one that would terminate American jurisdiction over Panamanian territory, and would introduce extensive modifications, to Panama's benefit, of the regime under which the canal is operated and defended. Henry Kissinger, as early as 1974, agreed with the Panamanian authorities on the principles which should lie at the basis of a new treaty. Since then Mr. Ellsworth Bunker has been laboring, with admirable patience and in the face of many vacillations and misgivings at home, at negotiations with the Panamanians for a new settlement.

The nature of the opposition in this country to a new arrangement based on the principles just mentioned flows of course from the feeling that it was this country that built the canal, paid for it, and has operated and protected it effectively for nearly three quarters of a century; that this arrangement has worked to the benefit of all concerned, and not least the Panamanians themselves; and that there is no reason to contemplate changes that would weaken the foundations on which this creditable achievement has rested. Opposed to this is the view that the arrangement in question is essentially a colonial one which, like other arrangements of that nature, has outlived its usefulness; that it is offensive to the Latin American community as a whole — so much so that it has ceased to be just a bilateral question but is counterproductive from the standpoint of our Latin American policy generally; that the Panamanians feel so violently about it that if no agreement can be achieved by negotiation they will soon resort to violence of one sort or another, with all the complications this would involve; and that, finally, in the view of Mr. Bunker himself, it would be "difficult if not impossible" for this country to continue to operate the canal in coming years against Panamanian opposition. In support of this latter view, which seems to have prevailed in Washington to this point, it is argued that the United States could well live with a settlement whereby all American jurisdiction over Panamanian territory would be abandoned, as would the indefinite validity of the agreements providing for an American military presence at the canal, it being understood that the new arrangements would be subject to renegotiation within a given period, and that the Panamanian government, meanwhile, would share in the benefits, as well as the administration and defense of the waterway. To such an arrangement, embodying as it does the principles to which Mr. Kissinger once agreed, the Panamanian government, it is argued, would presumably agree.

Each of these conflicting positions has logic and persuasiveness — so much so that, if taken as incompatible alternatives, they grow at once to the stature of a real dilemma. The question is whether they really have to be taken entirely as incompatible alternatives. It is my own conclusion that they do not — that the most promising solution would accept some elements of both views.

The awkwardness of attempting to continue to operate the canal under the existing arrangement, in the face of the passionate opposition of the Panamanians themselves and of the remainder of the Latin American states, not to mention the majority in the United Nations Assembly, is obvious. It could scarcely fail to lead to conflicts of a violent nature, in which we would automatically be cast, in

[54]

the world's eyes, in the role of "imperialists," and which would therefore play into the hands of our most savage detractors on the world scene, of whom we have a number. This we must concede to the advocates of change.

On the other hand one can only quail at the prospect of attempting to operate and protect the canal in some sort of "partnership" with the Panamanians. An arrangement of this nature would weaken the American position without giving permanent and complete satisfaction to the Panamanians. It would be replete with possibilities for disagreement and minor conflict. The United States authorities would find themselves pinched at many points between their commitment to the efficient operation of the waterway, on the one hand, and conflicting Panamanian desiderata (which the Panamanians would then have a right to bring forward), on the other. The American personnel of the enterprise, now numbering some 3,500 persons, without dependents, would lose much of their sense of personal security, with corresponding detriment to their morale and commitment.

Could not the dilemma be better resolved, one wonders, by turning the canal over entirely to the Panamanians? The proposal may sound extreme. But let us look at it in detail.

The canal is now in many respects a declining asset. In 1940, 50 percent of U.S. intercoastal trade passed through it. Now, only 3 percent does. Of the 13,875 ships that went through it in 1975, less than 10 percent (1,097 would appear to be the figure) were American. With the general rise in the size of ocean shipping, there are now floating (or about to float) on the high seas something around 3,000 ships which, for reasons of size, either cannot use the canal at all (this is true of well over a thousand) or can do so only with temporary modifications. There can be no question but that the proportion of shipping that cannot, or prefers not to, use the waterway will increase in the future.

If press reports are correct, only two major United States warships used the canal in 1975. In the entire period 1971–1975, it was used, in fact, only by twelve small American naval vessels. It is unavailable, for different reasons in each case, to the aircraft carriers and to the nuclear submarines.

In general, while the figure vacillates from year to year, not more than 10 to 15 percent of American import-export tonnage passes through it, and much of this in non-American vessels.

So far as the value of the canal tolls is concerned, the United States would have nothing to lose by abandoning the canal entirely. Operational costs for the waterway have recently been exceeding revenues. The 1975 loss would appear to have been around $9 million; and the figure for 1976 was expected to be around $12.5 million. The loss must be expected to grow. To this must be added the $2.3 million which we have been paying annually to the Panamanians as rental.

It is true that in the case of the abandonment of the canal to Panama, the United States could not, and should not, place much confidence in its further reliability as a facility for use by American shipping, naval or commercial. It is maintained by some of the advocates of a new treaty envisaging joint use that the Panamanians could, if they had to, operate it quite effectively and reliably. Anyone may believe this who will. American policy-makers must be excused if they prefer to see the proof of it in practice. The experience of the Suez Canal, which was closed to all traffic for eight of the twenty years it has been in the hands of the Egyptians, and denied, for political reason, to some traffic for almost all of that time, is not encouraging in this respect. Even if the first years of operation under Panamanian management should be satisfactory, the United States government could never place the same sort of confidence in the reliability of the waterway, or encourage American private enterprise to do so, that it placed before.

On the contrary, this government would be wise, should the canal be abandoned to the Panamanians, to discourage any extensive dependence upon it by American shippers, even to the point of making partial compensation to those shippers for use of the longer route around South America and encouraging the development of alternative facilities, for which a number of possibilities exist. The average extra cost for a ship of making the passage around South America, instead of through the canal, is reckoned at about $50,000. It is my own estimate that just out of the savings that would be effected by abandoning operation of the canal, and not counting defense costs, the United States could afford to make up half of the extra cost of circumnavigating South America for about six hundred vessels a year.

As alternatives: facilities for rapid handling of container traffic by rail from Texan ports to Southern California could pick up part of the load, as could similar facilities operating across southern Mexico. Bulk cargoes tend to lend themselves to shipment around South America in larger vessels which would in any case not use the canal.

If there were any financial sacrifice involved, it would be, in fact, on the side of the Panamanians. They have not been doing at all badly under the existing arrangements. It is generally estimated that 30 to 40 percent of their foreign exchange earnings, about 33 percent of their budgetary revenues, some 25 percent of their GNP, and 20 percent of their employment can be traced, one way or another, to the operation and defense of the canal by the United States. If they find this arrangement onerous and offensive, and think they could do better without it, this is their own affair. My only hope would be that the United States government would not, in this case, feel itself under obligation to make up any resulting deficits. Panama would be receiving the facility itself, which it would cost billions to replace, as a gift. Many Panamanians, particularly among the younger generation, have been vehement in their demands that the United States relinquish the canal to Panama and leave the scene. One must assume that they have taken the financial consequences into account.

The strongest opposition to turning the canal over to Panama would come, no doubt, from our defense establishment and those who serve as its spokesmen in our public life. The Army would not take kindly to the idea of abandoning its thirteen bases there; it seldom likes to abandon bases anywhere. The Navy, too, could be depended upon to squawk vigorously at the thought of losing its assured privilege of using a waterway which it now seldom uses, anyway. Similar complaints would come from all those who share in the spin-off from the American military presence in the Canal Zone.

To this, it must be said, first, that a certain diminution of the U.S. military presence will presumably be called for in any case, under the new treaty arrangements now in contemplation; and the remainder of it must be expected to constitute an endless bone of contention. But more important still is the recognition that the United States, once it had abandoned the canal and the Zone, would have no need of a presence there to assure the defense of the waterway. In the case of any attempt by another great power to seize it and convert it to its own purposes, it would be a very minor operation for the United States to assure the inoperability of the canal for as long as this was necessary.

It may be argued that all this would not be much more agreeable to the Panamanians than the arrangement they are now putting up with, and that other Latin American states, also, would find it a cause for grumbling. That may well be. But surely, at some point, people must be asked to accept the consequences of their own demands in this world. They cannot indefinitely have it both ways. They cannot both demand that Yankee go home, and then reproach him for doing so. The retirement of the United States from the canal and all that hangs together with it has been the indignant demand of the whole Latin American community for years on end. If the United States should find it advantageous at this point (and it is my own belief that it would) to yield to this demand, it would be acting on a sober and realistic judgment of its own interests. The demand must be presumed to have reflected a similar judgment on the part of those who raised it. The consequences for Panama would not, in the circumstances, be a responsibility of the United States.

2. CUBA

In early 1975 the United States, and with it that portion of the Latin American community which had not yet made its peace with Cuba, was moving rapidly towards a normalization of relations with that country. By midsummer the process was close to completion. The Organization of American States, at its meeting of the end of July, lifted the embargo and removed the sanctions that had been in force for some years against Cuba — and all this with the approval of the United States.

This action seems to have met with little interest on Castro's side. His response, in any case, was to prepare and carry out, within a matter of weeks after the OAS decision, the dispatch of several thousand Cuban troops to Angola, to assist the leaders of a single Marxist faction there to defeat the rival resistance movements and to fasten its own dictatorial control upon the helpless population of that vast territory.

The background of this extraordinary procedure remains obscure. Available evidence suggests that the move was made at Cuban, not Soviet, initiative — which is not to say that it was initially disagreeable to Moscow. Moscow may well have preferred to see the Cubans shoulder this unpleasant task rather than to accept either of the possible alternatives: one, a defeat of the Cuban-aided faction, which had long enjoyed Soviet support; the other, the use of Soviet forces, with all the international repercussions that would have involved. But Castro's own motives have never been revealed. Prominent among them must surely have been the desire to give combat training to his expeditionary forces, with a view to their possible later employment in the Western Hemisphere.

This procedure, in any case, was not reassuring in the light it shed on the attitude of the Castro regime towards its international obligations and towards its Latin American neighbors in particular. When the United States abandoned the Monroe Doctrine, it did so with the understanding that any effort by a non–Western Hemisphere power to intervene by force of arms in the internal affairs of a Latin American state would now be the concern of the Organization of American States in its entirety. This seems to me to imply that any similar intervention by a Latin American country in the affairs of a non–Western Hemisphere state would also be a matter of general Latin American interest, particularly because intervention sometimes invites counterintervention. Yet this dispatch of Cuban forces to Southern Africa was prepared, and its implementation undertaken, so far as I am aware, in deepest secrecy and without consultation with any other Latin American state. Plainly, other things appeared more important to Fidel Castro in that summer of 1975 than the normalization of Cuba's relations with her American neighbors.

These events dealt a severe blow to the prospects for a better Cuban-American relationship; and so long as Cuban forces participate in civil struggle or in internal police activities in Angola it is clear that no further progress can be made. Situations of this nature, however, seldom last forever, if only because the presence of foreign troops in any country, especially for active purposes of the sort just mentioned, is not normally agreeable for very long either to the inhabitants or to the native rulers. Someday, presumably, the Cubans will have to come home (having learned a few things, let us hope, from experience); and when they do, the question of United States relations with the Castro regime will again come onto the docket.

It is of course premature to suggest what our course should be at that time. But there are two things, one of which even has its implications for the present moment, that might well be borne in mind in connection with the problem that will then face us.

First: if the United States expects to handle effectively, over a long period of time, its relations with a pseudo-Communist Cuba, its first concern must be to place itself in an advantageous position for doing so. This, however, will not be accomplished before it detaches itself from its cloying and confusing association with the anti-Castro Cuban exiles. This applies not just to the State Department, but to the Defense Department and to the American intelligence community generally.

One does not need to stress the damage done to American interests by the Bay of Pigs episode, or to evoke the suspicions that continue to surround the assassination of President John Kennedy, to make the point that intimacy with the Cuban exiles has proved unfortunate for this country in a whole series of instances.

If one were to attempt to list the causes for the signal failures of American policy in the postwar period, a prominent place on the list would have to be given, in fact, to our frequent inability to find a proper relationship to people whom we conceive, often on rather flimsy evidence, to be our political and ideological friends. We cope well enough with our enemies; where we fail is with our friends. Especially has this been true since the Cold War brought us into a situation of apparent companionship with numbers of people with whom, in other respects, we have very little in common. All sorts of people — Chinese Nationalists, Vietnamese, Persians, Croatians, Ukrainians, Spaniards, what you will — have claimed intimacy with us on the basis of a common anticommunism; and they have often succeeded in bending us to their purposes, sometimes with important help from domestic-American lobbies, by taking advantage of our simplistic single-mindedness, our tendency to lose ourselves in fascination with a single issue, the difficulty we seem to have in recognizing contradictory values in a given situation and then finding our way thoughtfully among them.

Just so — the Cuban exiles. It is not to suggest that they are bad people to point out that their interests are not our interests. Their purposes are not our purposes. The two, on occasion, may overlap; but they never coincide entirely. Yet these people have succeeded in selling themselves repeatedly to the American intelligence community, often on the basis of a claimed expertise that is as specious as it is untrustworthy; and in this way they have whipsawed us on more than one occasion to their liking.

This is why the first requirement of a proper stance from which to approach the problem of relations with Castro's Cuba, when the moment again arrives for exploration of the more constructive possibilities of this relationship, is to disembarrass ourselves of this association and to restore thereby the freedom of action, and the integrity, of our own policy.

Secondly, we will do well, when that pleasant day comes, to sharpen and harden our understanding of the meaning and implication of diplomatic recognition, as an act of policy. We have allowed the impression to gain currency, particularly during the long years of nonrecognition of Soviet Russia and then of Communist China, that the naming of an American ambassador to another country constitutes some sort of patent of American approval for the nature of the regime in power there. One could perhaps find a modicum of justification for such a view in the fact that long ago, in the days when diplomacy was primarily dynastic, diplomatic recognition usually implied the acceptance of the legitimacy of the royal dynasty to which it was extended. But by and large, the conditions of the modern age require that diplomatic representation should be viewed not as an act of moral judgment but as a normal convenience of international life — a useful channel of communication between governments, unrelated to their liking for each other, their approval or disapproval of the other's political system, or the degree of their agreement on specific political questions. Channels of communication are required, after all, for the transmission of unpleasant messages as well as pleasant ones. There are times when it is useful to be able to communicate through orderly and established channels even with a regime for which one has nothing but abhorrence.

One can understand, of course, that there may be situations where the dispatch of a full-fledged ambassador, requiring as it normally does his being personally received by the foreign head of state and muttering a few polite platitudes on this occasion, may seem more in the way of deference than one wishes to pay to the regime in question. In this case, there is always the institution of de facto recogni-

[62]

tion to fall back upon. One need not, just to provide a proper channel of communication, have full diplomatic representation at the
ambassadorial level. One can accredit a chargé d'affaires, who can
be, and normally is, a person of lower rank and prestige.

One wishes at times that the United States government would
show itself better aware of the advantages of this useful device. On a
number of occasions this government has gone directly from a state of
no recognition at all to one of full ambassadorial representation, or
vice versa, when de facto relations would have been the better solution. A change in relations with Cuba might well be a point where
this distinction could usefully be borne in mind.

And there is, in this connection, a worse danger still. Not only
has it seemed to be the settled practice of the United States in recent
years to accredit a full-fledged ambassador to practically every
country that becomes a member of the United Nations, but it also
seems to have been accepted as *de rigueur*, especially in the case of
smaller states, that, this step having once been taken, it must at once
be followed up by a variety of aid programs. So widely is this principle accepted that even the American press seems dominated by it
and frequently confuses the two things, treating the establishment of
diplomatic relations as though it were something from which economic or military assistance, or both, would normally flow.

Whatever may have been the justification for this assumption in
other instances, there is none in the case of Castro's Cuba. The Castro regime has done reasonably well without us for many years. We
have done equally well without it. It has even taught us a useful lesson in demonstrating that dependence by a smaller country on the
Soviet Union for economic and developmental aid does not necessarily lead to utter catastrophe for us.

Whatever motives may lead Señor Castro, at some future date, to
seek a better relationship with us, if that time and situation ever arrive, we may be sure that those motives will not include any very
friendly or respectful feeling towards our country. For years on end
he has poured vilification on our heads, has done what he could to

[63]

disabuse his own people and others of any confidence they might otherwise have in our value as a society or our good faith as an international partner, and has preened himself, in the eyes of our worst enemies, with his hatred and defiance of our country. Such things should not be too suddenly forgotten. Whatever its failings, there comes a time when a country, like an individual, has to manifest some sense of its own dignity. Even if all the things Castro has said about us were true, it would not be well for us to profess too soon to forget them.

We would do well, in short, when the day for a more active policy towards Cuba arrives, to avoid histrionics and over-reaction. There are ways of dealing coolly, at arm's length, with a regime of this nature, neither forgetting the bitter lessons of the past nor precluding the possibility of future changes for the better. In international life, as occasionally in personal life, a distant but polite relationship avoids troubles that would not be avoided either by demonstrative hostility or by exaggerated attempts at intimacy.

There is one more possible source of confusion surrounding Cuban-American relations about which I would like to say a word of warning. A number of Americans have recently returned from Cuba favorably impressed, in a number of respects, with what they have seen there: with evident improvements in the lot of the people at large, with the degree of support the regime appears to enjoy, with the absence of Soviet-type security precautions, with the relaxed and friendly way they themselves were received. It is hard to judge the accuracy of these reports, but they have been so frequently heard that one is obliged to suppose that the general picture they convey is a correct one.

Some of the American press, in relaying and commenting upon these reports, has contrived to convey the suggestion that should it really be true that the Castro regime has important positive achievements to its credit, this would mean that we, in some way, had been wrong all along; that our position with relation to Cuba had been misconceived; that this was proof of the justice of Castro's cause, of the wrong-headedness of our own, and of great error in the shaping of American policy.

I can see no justification for such a conclusion. Our conflict with Castro's Cuba has not been over the merits of a given form of government; it has been over the behavior of a neighboring state in its relations with us and with others.

But beyond this, the reasoning I have just referred to reflects a misconception that will bedevil us in more instances than just that of Cuba if we continue to lend ourselves to it. Even if the rosiest of these views of Communist Cuba are correct, this is not the heart of the problem. This would not be the first time, nor will it be the last, that a regime organized on principles irreconcilable with our own and bitterly committed against us in world politics has produced creditable results in the administration of the society subject to its authority. Not all dictatorships are greatly successful in the social sense, but there is nothing to say they cannot be. The Maoist order of Chinese society was one that commanded the almost dithyrambic enthusiasm of a large number of American visitors. This does not alter the fact that it was a regime based on principles totally at odds with our own, and that it conducted over the course of many years, like the Castro regime in Cuba, the most savage sort of campaign of defamation against our country.

The fact that other regimes, highly distasteful to us, have successes in the development of the societies they direct does not prove them right and us wrong in our mutual relationship. There is, as was noted above, a price to be paid for democratic liberties. Part of this price may be the necessity of standing by and watching certain things being done better elsewhere than they are in our own country. This may be a good reason for a searching critical review of the soundness of some of our own procedures. It is not a reason for holding ourselves at fault in such differences as we may have with the regimes in question on the diplomatic level. If we estabish, as the decisive criterion for our relations with other governments, not the nature of their domestic-political principles and practices but rather

[65]

the nature of their behavior towards us and the world community as participants in world affairs, we will not fall victim to the sort of confusion I have just described. We will then neither decline to deal with another regime just because its internal institutions are repugnant to us, nor will we feel ourselves obliged to have pleasant dealings with it just because it achieves certain creditable internal results, if its behavior towards us does not meet the minimum standards of friendly international intercourse.

3. CONCLUSIONS

Our relations with the remainder of Latin America involve, of course, a host of problems, most of them minor, some a bit more than that. Of these, the most serious are no doubt those that concern the prices for Latin American food and raw materials on the United States market. Here is a point at which we could probably ease our relations with a number of these countries, though, as so often happens, only at the cost of overcoming a certain amount of domestic-political resistance. What would seem to be needed is not a system of concealed subsidies established by the fixing of prices regularly higher than the market would normally bear, but rather the assurance over long periods of time of stable prices reasonably close to what the market could normally be expected to yield. Whether these would in all cases have to be established by agreement with the countries concerned is questionable. It would be preferable, on principle, that they be established unilaterally, by action of our government, but at levels clearly fair and acceptable to the producing countries. This, in any case, would seem to be one area where the United States could act effectively to remove one of the most serious psychological burdens that rest on its relations with the countries of this hemisphere.

Beyond this, however — beyond, that is, the regularization of our relations with Cuba and Panama, and beyond whatever we could do in this question of the prices for Latin American food and raw materials — there is no reason to exert ourselves beyond a point in the development of our relations with the countries of that region, particularly those of South America. The cultural differences are great. In many respects, their peoples are more closely connected, traditionally, culturally, and sometimes even commercially, with Western Europe than with ourselves. Americans are not very popular, by and large, in those parts; and I can see no very good reason why they need be. The less we fuss over these countries, the less we burden them with our presence, the less we interest ourselves in their affairs, the better we will be regarded, and the less strained will be the relationship generally.

Many years ago, returning from a journey through certain of the countries of South America, I pleaded with the State Department to urge our representatives there to "relax — leave them alone." I have seen no reason to depart from the view then stated. Beyond the questions of Cuba and Panama, and of the security generally of Central America, we have no really vital interests in that part of the world. Let us be generous in small things, courteous in all circumstances, and helpful wherever we can be, but beyond that not greatly concerned for their opinion of us, and happy enough not to be an active factor in their affairs. The rest, surely, will look after itself.

IV

Africa

I. GENERAL

With respect to a continent where there is so much variety among governments both in nature and in behavior, all generalizations are dangerous; and the thoughts I am about to express, if taken as generalizations, will also have validity only within certain limits. But it was my impression, when traveling in Africa a few years ago, that in its approach to these black African states, most of them new ones on the political topography of the world, official Washington had been acting under the infuence of some sort of massive guilt complex, or feeling of moral inferiority — a state of mind which led many people to feel that it was *we*, in the first instance, who had to prove our benevolence towards the peoples in question, we who had to win their favor, rather than the other way around. It was as though it were we who were the only losers if relations did not work out to everyone's satisfaction. And the result, it seemed to me, was a persistent overdoing of many things: of aid programs, of diplomatic representation, of the size and activity of official American staffs, of entertainment, of the sending out of high-ranking delegations and public figures, and so on. We seemed to feel obliged to suggest aid programs where none was seriously requested or valued. We sent ambassadors where there was no real justification for their presence. We turned the other cheek to slights and other forms of offensive behavior — a practice that befits a great power, to be sure, up to a certain point, but becomes undesirable when carried too far, if only because it encourages assumptions and states of mind on the other side which are in the long run not tolerable. We allowed to come into existence, in other words, an atmosphere of the relationship that placed us in the position of the anxious suitor, always prepared to accept today's rebuff in the hope of tomorrow's favor.

Do I exaggerate? Possibly, particularly in the case of some of the West African countries, where self-confidence and sense of security are greater, where there is normally less strain in the relationship, and where neither they nor we have the urge to over-react. Perhaps, too, things have changed since my visit. Perhaps time and experience have to some extent mitigated these tendencies. But that the evidences of them can still be found in the reactions of American officialdom, at home and abroad, is surely the case.

It is not easy to uncover the sources of this curious state of mind. It is of course one that relates not just to the new states of Africa; it pervades the American approach to the Third World generally. Its causes are obviously multiple. To some extent it probably reflects the power over the American mind of the syndrome, mentioned above, of the virtue of small states and the wickedness of large ones. There is also, one senses, the influence of the missionaries, whose aim is normally to cling to their presence in these places at all costs, and who are in a position to bring heavy pressures to bear on Washington. There is the similar influence of the so-called expatriates, people concerned to protect their life and residence in foreign countries, even at the cost of much indulgence of the local regimes. There is also, no doubt, the influence of the black vote in the United States — a factor which commands the respect of legislators even when it is not actively exerted. There is still, perhaps to a lesser extent than some years ago, the fear that in the absence of all this scrambling for African favor from the American side the Russians might move in and preempt the positions we would like to retain. There are the occupational interests of a considerable body of aid administrators and informational officers whose jobs, and sometimes the importance and weight of whose agencies, depend on the continuation of the programs in which they are involved. There is, finally, the influence of the liberal press at home, always ready to suspect the United States of lack of liberality in its treatment of smaller powers.

All these factors probably play a part. But beyond them there seems to be something deeper and more difficult of definition: some inner insecurity that affects Americans when they come into contact with smaller and less developed societies — something that causes them to confuse respect with popularity, and to feel that if popularity is not forthcoming, it is they who are somehow at fault.

However that may be, it is a tendency that has often had unfortunate results. Not only has it often misled others as to the real elements of our position, but it has laid us open to a wide variety of forms of blackmail, some delicate, some not so delicate, some minor, others serious both in scale and in offensiveness. Worst of all, it defeats itself, for it encourages others to take our benevolence for granted and to assume that they need make no reciprocal concessions to retain it. The first requirement for getting on with most foreign peoples is to demonstrate that you are quite capable of getting on without them. An overeagerness to please suggests the opposite.

2. SOUTHERN AFRICA

The most important immediate problems for American policy in Africa are, of course, those that relate to the so-called white-ruled countries of the southern part of that continent.

The story of our present involvement began with Angola. There is much to be said about the events that led up to this involvement; and it is a temptation to dwell on them. Certainly no metropolitan power of recent times was ever so unjustly treated in Western opinion as were the Portuguese in their earlier relationship to this region. Those members of the Western press and officialdom who pressed so hard for their relinquishment of Angola and Mozambique might well ask themselves, in the light of conditions in those places today, whether they, in their desire to demonstrate the fervent quality of their liberal idealism, did not play fast and loose with the interests of the respective native populations.

All this, however, is water over the dam. Those populations are now having to experience the drastic decline in economic and other conditions which was, in the circumstances, to be expected. There is nothing any of us can do about it, except perhaps to ponder the lessons it suggests.

Mr. Kissinger's reason for being concerned about the situation in Angola was, in any case, not this. What bothered him was his impression that the outcome of the struggle for power among the various resistance groups which attended the Portuguese departure from Angola was an important victory for the Russians, that they were now riding high in a place where our own efforts to win influence had failed, and that there was a danger, as things stood, that the same unfortunate sequence of events would now take place in Rhodesia.

I am not at all sure that this view of the situation in Angola is correct. The Russians had been supporting the MPLA* for some years before the final denouement, just as we had been supporting rival elements. *Their* faction then suddenly showed signs of winning — certainly to their surprise, possibly to their consternation. But one cannot disavow a faction just because it suddenly succeeds. The

* *Movimento Popular para a Libertação de Angola.*

consolidation of MPLA power over most of the territory, with Cuban support, may — as mentioned above — have seemed preferable, from the Russian standpoint, to any of the visible alternatives. So they supported that faction with massive — too massive — arms shipments. Whether they are fully pleased with the result is another matter. They had certainly been successful in indoctrinating the MPLA leaders with a number of nasty qualities, including an unshakable ideological self-righteousness, a thoroughgoing hatred of us, and a high degree of bloody-mindedness with relation to anyone who disagreed with them or questioned their aspirations for dictatorial power in Angola. It is less certain that the Russians have succeeded in instilling into those same people any great affection for, or loyalty to, the Soviet Union, or any high degree of reliability as agents for Russian influence and power in that part of the world.

I sometimes wonder whether Mr. Kissinger fully understood the embarrassments and limitations even of Soviet power in regions far from the shadows of the Soviet armed forces. Gratitude is not an outstanding quality either of African guerrilla leaders or of Cuban mercenaries. To cause such people to pursue interests other than their own, as they see them, would take more in the way of a Russian military presence than the Russians are willing to invest on this slippery terrain.

There is no reason, furthermore, to suppose that the Russians are pleased over the effect Angolan events have had in bringing the United States to an active role in that part of the world. It is most unlikely that they either foresaw this or wanted it.

However that may be, Mr. Kissinger's impressions of what had occurred in Angola did, as mentioned, cause him to intervene in the Rhodesian situation with pressures on the white Rhodesian regime to make concessions to the more moderate of its black African opponents with a view to the eventual achievement of "majority rule."

It is not easy to judge the usefulness of this intervention. The racial policies of the Rhodesian regime differ greatly from those of their South African neighbors. In particular, they are not based in any way on the principles of *apartheid*. In some respects they are considerably more liberal than the Western newspaper reader would suppose. In other respects they have long appeared, and continue to appear, to Western visitors as unjust, unjustified, and unwise. The situation has now deteriorated considerably; and it is questionable whether the Rhodesian whites could save themselves, in the sense of buying a tolerable and secure future for themselves in Rhodesia, by hasty last-minute concessions. Their greatest hope, for the moment, continues to lie in their own unity and military strength, such as it is, in contrast to the chronic disunity of their opponents, but then only if that strength is accompanied by a readiness on their part to move towards the creation of a more mature and hopeful political system, wherever this is possible without exposing them to the dangers of total destruction or expulsion.

Outside pressures, in such circumstances, can be useful; and those of Mr. Kissinger have perhaps been a good thing, as far as they went. But at the moment of writing the leaders of the African countries around Rhodesia have withdrawn their support from the more moderate black Rhodesian leaders within the country, who have been at least in touch with the present Rhodesian government, and have conferred that support on the more radical outside resistance leaders, who are pressing for a military showdown. There already are, and will continue to be, demands that the U.S. government should, in the name of an enthusiasm for "majority rule," do the same.

Here, great caution is in order. There is no evidence that these outside leaders command the confidence of a majority of the black population within the country. Such evidence as exists suggests that their more moderate rivals come, if anything, closer to doing so. The demand is, in effect, that a monopoly of power be at once conferred on these outside leaders, on no stronger a justification than their own assertion that they are the people who ought to possess it. What would follow, should this be done, would no doubt be rule *in the name of a* majority. This is not the same as majority rule.

Nor is there any reason to suppose that a tolerable place would be left, under a radical black dictatorship, for the white population, and that countries elsewhere would not be asked to cope with a massive exodus of these people. Is the United States prepared to accept them, to care for them, and to provide them with a new life? If not, would it not be taking upon itself a heavy responsibility, at the expense of others, by encouraging a solution that might well lead to their expulsion?

Surely, the best course for the United States is a reserved neutrality with relation to the internal conflicts of this unfortunate country, coupled with a readiness to be of practical assistance wherever this would offer chances of moderating passions and restraining bloodshed. Beyond this, there lie only the abundant pitfalls of attempting to strike noble poses with relation to a situation one did not create, cannot remove, and understands very poorly.

The situation in the great arid territory of Southwest Africa is something else again. The United Nations majority has been pressing the South Africans, for many years, to relinquish their hold on this territory and to grant independence to its inhabitants. Meanwhile, guerrilla forces, organized under the aegis of something called SWAPO,* enjoying considerable Communist and Western-liberal support, and much encouraged by events in neighboring Angola, have come into action with attacks from outside against the borders of the territory. The South African government, for reasons of its own, has recently shown a readiness to give the territory its independence. It is willing to transfer sovereign power to a body of elected leaders of the various tribes of the region. It is not willing to transfer it to the self-appointed leaders of the outside guerrilla forces. This,

* South West African People's Organization.

of course, does not suit the latter at all. Their claim to be the legitimate rulers of the territory, and the ones to whom absolute power ought to be turned over at once, is, again, one that rests solely on their own say-so; but it is one that they are not willing to compromise by any accommodations with tribal leaders elected under South African authority.

One is constrained to wonder what "independence" could mean, even in the best of circumstances, for this curiously constructed territory. That it would spell economic disaster for the African natives, and this on a scale even greater than in the former Portuguese territories, seems certain; for the South Africans, whatever may be their other failings, have poured developmental support into Southwest Africa on a scale far greater than most of the black African countries to the north have ever received from all sources put together; and this, presumably, the inhabitants will have to go without as soon as their independence becomes a fact.

But beyond this, one has difficulty picturing this territory as a single political entity, governing itself. There is no such thing as a Southwest African people. Least of all is there any such thing as a "Namibian" people. (The name "Namibia" is an invention of the outside guerrilla leaders, together with their friends at the UN. Most people within the territory have never heard of it.) What does exist is a number of tribes, grouped around a vast central-western semi-desert, sometimes at great distance one from another. There has been very little intercommunication among them; and they have little in common. The appearance in the midst of any of them of a person of different tribal identity, in the guise of an official of an independent "Namibia," would be something to which they would not readily become accustomed.

It is, I suppose, not impossible that someday some semblance of an indigenous government might be created among these tribes; something like this has happened, I know, in other parts of Africa where the boundaries, representing former colonial delineations, were not much less artificial. That this could happen, however, on the basis of some peaceful consensus, seems doubtful. It would be more likely to be the achievement of some sort of dictatorship established by force of arms. Most unlikely of all is that any of this would result in any appreciable betterment of the situation of the native population, economically or politically.

We will be pressed, no doubt, by the UN majority, and possibly by some of the missionary elements, to support the consignment of power over the territory to the outside guerrilla leaders. It is hard to see any reason why we should submit to this sort of pressure, or why, indeed, we should take any position at all with regard to the future of the territory. Here, again, we do not have the answers.

We come then to the central problem of the region, which is South Africa itself.

I hope that nothing I am about to say will be taken as an apology for the racial policies of the South African government. A number of these policies commend themselves no better to me than they do to a great many other Western visitors to that country. I, like others, have tried where I could, in my visits to South Africa, to put in my word of warning against their possible consequences. So far as I am concerned, the South African government, like the Rhodesian one, has made its own bed. It, too, must lie in it.

The Western press, in its treatment of South African affairs, contrives to give several impressions which represent at best dangerous oversimplifications of the situation there, and which are not helpful as an approach to the problems involved for American policy.

One might think, to read much of this material, that the majority of the black African population of South Africa stood squarely behind the extremists in their demands for early and violent action in the event there is no great change in governmental policies. This is nowhere proven. Unhappiness there is, in abundance. Desire for all the miseries of a civil war? Most doubtful.

One might suppose, to read these Western reports, that there had been no recent change for the better in the policies and practices of the South African authorities. Again — incorrect. There have been improvements of some significance — forced, if you will, by pressure — but improvements nonetheless.

One might also suppose, reading this material, that if the whites did not at once give over, they would assuredly be crushed by the black or non-white majority, supported by the rest of black Africa. Also a questionable assumption. The position of these South African whites is far more powerful than that of their counterparts in Rhodesia. They are some fifteen times more numerous, excellently armed, well organized, and by nature extremely stubborn. A civil war there might be, but one of such bloodiness that there would, as a consequence of it, be no victors — only losers.

One could also suppose that all the whites had to do, to assure to themselves a safe and happy future, would be to yield at once to the demands for the abandonment of *apartheid* and the introduction of "majority rule." Actually, this would mean an enormous upheaval, which would shake the country to its foundations. Who knows what the consequences would be? Perhaps it is too late for the whites to rescue much of their position in this way. We, in any case, cannot know.

Finally, those in the West who feel most violently about this whole situation often contrive to suggest that a total defeat — destruction or expulsion — of the whites, while a drastic expedient, would at least open up to the majority of the population hopeful prospects for a pleasant democratic future. Wrong again. The tragedy of South Africa lies precisely in the fact that neither of these two great bodies of its inhabitants, the whites and the non-whites, could have a tolerable existence, as things stand today, without the other. This is not like other African countries. It has a very highly developed, sophisticated economy, the productivity of which alone permits so large a number of people to live on this relatively arid plateau as now inhabit it. The whites are dependent on the non-white labor. The non-whites are dependent on white expertise in technology and management. Without both these contributions the economy could not be maintained.

For all these reasons, abrupt and violent changes, however they may appeal to the heated imaginations of Western liberals, are not the answers. Nor are empty gestures.

The United States government will continue to be pressed to compel American firms to withdraw from their business connections with South Africa. This is a silly suggestion. The blacks of that country themselves do not want it. The foreign firms operating branches in that country have stood in the forefront of the effort to achieve better treatment, both in wages and in responsibility of function, for black workers; and they have had some success. Nothing would be gained by their removal.

Even sillier are the demands that one should retaliate against *apartheid* by refusing to permit South African athletes to compete in international competition. Aside from the fact that one would be punishing the wrong people, such demands tend simply to heighten the isolation of South Africa from the main currents of world opinion; and that is precisely what anyone interested in the improvement of conditions there ought to be concerned to avoid. The extremisms of *apartheid* were ones that could have been conceived and pursued only in a country already suffering from too much isolation.

Demands such as these, addressed to the United States government, are not really demands for useful and hopeful action with relation to the situation in South Africa. They are demands for the striking of high-minded and heroic poses, like those of the persons who raise the demands in the first place. The United States government has no need to strike such poses. The problems in question are not its problems. It does not have the answers to them. There is little it can do to be useful today. Perhaps someday greater opportunities for usefulness will open up. But the United States government will be able to take advantage of those opportunities only if it has, in the meantime, observed a wise and impartial reserve, refrained from any demonstrative taking-of-sides, and contrived in this way to retain some measure of the goodwill and confidence of all the factions involved.

V

The Near East

ASSUMING THE UNDUE DEPENDENCE ON THE ARAB AND IRANIAN OIL TO have been removed, would the United States have any vital interest in the Near East?* (Please bear in mind that this question contains the word "vital," which ought not to be used lightly.)

I cannot see that the United States could be said to have any such interest. The oil? Not once the dependence was ended. The Suez Canal? A trivial factor. The waterway was closed for eight of the twenty years it has been under Egyptian control. Our vital interests were not affected. Its unreliability, so long as it remains under Egyptian control, is such (as would be the case of a Panama Canal under Panamanian control) that we ought not to permit ourselves to develop any significant degree of dependence upon it in any case.

Our commitment to Israel? Is this a vital interest? It is unquestionably a serious one, but vital? Not if we are going to stick to the strict meaning of that term. If the worst were to happen there, this

* I know it to be the prevailing fashion to term everything east of Libya as the "Middle East." What, in this case, the "East" would be, or the "Near East," I cannot picture to myself. I propose in any case, as an old-fashioned person, to refer to the area from Libya to (and, for purposes of convenience in this discussion, including) Iran as the Near East, which seems to me to be the proper designation.

would come as a tremendous shock to American and world opinion, but it would not bring mortal damage to our national life in the physical sense.

That we have a serious interest in the fate of the state of Israel is clear. When we lent our support, nearly thirty years ago, to its establishment, and this in a part of the world the inhabitants of which had never given their assent to such a development, we accepted a certain share of the responsibility for the success of the undertaking, at least in its initial stages. This was not a commitment in perpetuity. No American administration would have had the right to commit our policy in perpetuity to responsibility for the security of a territory, not part of the United States, situated thousands of miles from our shores. Indeed, that is something no sovereign state could expect of any other.

I am not suggesting that we should now withdraw our interest in the endurance and the security of the state of Israel. On the contrary, I think this interest must be recognized as a serious one. I am fully aware of, and indeed share personally in, the deep concern of a great part of American opinion for the survival and the prospering of this new state. I interpret this concern as a commitment of sorts — a commitment not to the Israelis but to ourselves — a commitment to do all in our power, short of the actual dispatch and employment of combat forces, to assure that Israel continues to exist — that its people are not destroyed, enslaved, or driven into the sea by hostile neighbors. This is a far-reaching commitment; but I think we must accept it.

We have one other serious interest in the Near East, and that is that the entire region not fall under the dominant influence or control of any great outside power. This could refer of course, in the circumstances, only to the Soviet Union. It is an interest that flows logically from the commitment to Israel, but not from that alone. It is a contingency that we would be concerned to avert, if only because of the wider destabilizing effects it would have, even if the problem of Israel did not exist.

[81]

It is, fortunately, not a very likely contingency. The people who see Russian forces streaming down into that region, occupying it in its entirety, and bringing it all under direct Soviet rule, have a poor understanding both of Russian aims and capabilities and of the normal embarrassments and limitations of great-power imperialism. The danger is thus more the product of some people's imaginations than of any real probability. But the impression of its reality has been assiduously and effectively peddled by those who choose to see no limits to Soviet capabilities and no restraints on Soviet ambition. So let us recognize this possibility, too, at least as a subjective product of the Western imagination, and accept it as a serious interest to see that this, too, our bad dream, does not take on flesh and blood.

We are left, then, with two major considerations that should guide us in shaping American policy towards this region. The first is that we must be prepared to do all in our power, short of direct military involvement, to prevent the destruction of the state of Israel. The second is that we must assure that no other great power comes to dominate the Near and Middle East as a whole. What does this mean in terms of American policy for these coming years?

It means of course, first and foremost, the termination of the dependence on Middle Eastern oil. I have already mentioned this in connection with our general position in world affairs. But a further word must be said about it in this specific connection.

It should be noted that what is required is not a total absence of imports of oil from the countries in question. There are, to be sure, some countries — notably Libya and Iraq — whose attitudes towards us and towards their responsibilities as members of the international community are of such offensiveness that one wonders why American firms were ever permitted to do business with them in the first place. (I am aware that Libyan and Iraqi oil would probably find its way into American refineries anyway, even if direct imports were stopped. But it seems to me that even a reasonable sense of national dignity would argue against putting great sums of American money directly into the hands of a man so inclined generally, and of such offensiveness in his attitude towards us, as Colonel Qaddafi has shown himself to be.) The effort might be made, it seems to me, to terminate entirely direct American imports from these countries. But with these exceptions, what is needed is only the reduction of our imports from the countries in question to a point where the degree of our dependence on them would not be serious and where we would thus have achieved, vis-à-vis their rulers, a bargaining power at least not inferior to their own. Until we do that, we will have no effective voice with them. I note with surprise press reports to the effect that President Carter expects to meet with the rulers of certain of these countries or their representatives and to discuss problems of the region with them. In what capacity, I wonder, would he approach them? As a supplicant? Why should they make any concessions to us, or even heed our views? They have us by the short hairs. They are already getting from us everything they want — more, in fact, than they can use — without making any concessions at all. No American President should ever approach other rulers from a position as humiliating as this.

These views reflect no hostility towards the countries in question, nor even any resentment over their action in raising the prices for oil as they have. We have invited it — with our inflation, our greed for oil, our willingness to accept a growing dependence in order to obtain it. They have done what appeared to them to be in *their* interests; it was up to us, not them, to look after *ours*.

I am also aware, in saying these things, that the effort to eliminate this dependence will not be an easy one. It will perhaps be easier than we think, if undertaken with determination and under effective leadership; but it will be nothing that can be combined with "business as usual." It will involve a major program, costly and demanding, such as might be mounted in wartime under the pressure of military necessity. It will involve much inconvenience, personal and political. But it is a major necessity, not a matter of choice.

There are those who will point out, in this connection, that it is

[83]

not just our own interests that we have to consider, in undertaking to reduce this dependence, but those of our NATO allies, who share in it. This is quite true. But the effort to arrive at some sort of coordinated action with them at the time of the Arab embargo was not successful. And actually, I can think of nothing we could do to help them that would be more effective than putting ourselves, first of all, in a position from which we could deal on equal terms with the oil producers. Until we do that, we cannot act effectively even in our interests, much less in theirs. Whether they choose to do the same (and it is greatly to be desired that they should) is primarily their affair.

A second thing we have to do is to bring about an early clarification — not just vis-à-vis the Israelis themselves but also vis-à-vis the Arabs — of the limits of our responsibility for Israeli policy. We have allowed the impression to become established throughout the entire region that we have it in our power to make the Israelis do almost anything we want, and that this being the case, we are really responsible for Israeli policy. This assumption is reflected in a host of Arab statements. It is, of course, wholly incorrect. Not only can we not dictate to the Israelis, who are very well aware of the strength of their bargaining power vis-à-vis us, but it is a real question whether we ought to do it even if we could. (More about that in a moment.)

We have compounded this error — of letting the Arabs hold us responsible for Israeli policy — by letting the Israelis look to us as their advocates and champions vis-à-vis the Arabs. Considering our helplessness in the face of the oil-producing states, this is even sillier.

What this all means is that we have allowed ourselves to be maneuvered into a position where each of the two parties believes it can use us for its own ends, where each has the impression that it is primarily through us that its desiderata can be achieved, with the result that we are always the first to be blamed, no matter whose ox is gored; and all this in a situation where we actually have very little influence with either party. Seldom, surely, can a great power have got itself into a more unsound and unneccessary position.

I have just indicated a doubt as to whether we should attempt to influence the Israelis even if we could. What I had in mind was influencing them on the specific questions in contention between them and their Arab neighbors over the terms of a permanent settlement. There are others, I know, including some who know much more about this region than I do, who will disagree. Mr. George Ball, for example, feels that we should first put forward our own specific proposals for a settlement, as we would like to see it, then solicit the agreement of the Russians and certain of our NATO allies, and then attempt to induce the parties to accept them.

I stand firmly with Mr. Ball on the need for an attempt to reach an understanding with the Soviet Union with relation to the larger problems of this region, but not on the details of a possible Arab-Israeli settlement. That, it seems to me, should be left for direct negotiation between Israel and her Arab neighbors. Our own role should be confined to assuring that the Israelis are strong enough militarily so that the idea of crushing them by force of arms does not offer promising prospects to anybody, and so that they have an adequate measure of bargaining power in any negotiations on these subjects they may enter into. But we should not try to tell them, or the Arabs, what the terms of a settlement should be. It is they, after all, not we, who would have to live with any settlement that might be achieved. Many of us can think, I am sure, of concessions which, in our personal opinion, it would be wise for the Israelis to make; but for the United States government to take the responsibility of urging them to make such concessions is quite another matter. There are many who would think, for example, that it would be wise for them to give up the Golan Heights. They may of course be right. But how can we be sure? What would our responsibility be if we urged this upon them and it turned out to be disastrous? It is the same problem, in principle, that we faced with the South Africans and the Rhodesians.

[85]

The fact that we need not have prior agreement with the Russians, or with anyone else, on the actual terms of a possible Israeli settlement does not mean that there is no need for a Soviet-American meeting of the minds about the wider problems of the Near East. What is needed is, first, a firm understanding that neither of the two powers will attempt to dominate the region and to exploit it against the interests of the other—that both, aside from promoting agreement between the Arabs and Israelis, will leave it generally alone; and secondly, that both are determined not to permit the troubles of that area to become a serious and dangerous source of conflict between them. Serious as are the questions at issue within the region itself, there is none of them that compares in importance with the necessity of avoiding military complications between the Soviet Union and the United States; indeed, it is hard to picture any circumstances in which the interests of the parties immediately involved — Arabs or Israelis — could really be served by the outbreak of such complications. The first duty of both the Soviet Union and the United States is to the preservation of world peace, not to the interests of their respective clients in the Near East. In pursuing such an understanding with the Soviet Union, we would of course have to explain to the Russians, and to ask them to accept, the nature and seriousness of our commitment to the endurance of the state of Israel. This would have to stand as a specific reservation to our commitment not to involve ourselves in the affairs of the region. But it should not, in view of its essentially defensive nature, be one difficult for the Russians to accept.

Under this concept the two great powers would, as chairmen of the Geneva talks, try to be helpful to the parties in coming to some agreement over the problems of boundaries and of Israel's future relations to her neighbors, but they would avoid intimate involvement in the negotiations, and would consult before making representations to the parties on individual points of difference.

There is one aspect of American policy where clarification would have to be achieved, and certain modifications introduced, before the United States would be in a favorable position to seek agreement with the Soviet Union along the lines just suggested. This refers to the heavy arms shipments to certain of the governments of the Near Eastern area.

It is to me little short of incomprehensible that so scant attention has been given in the United States to the effect upon the Russians of what the United States government has done in recent years in the sale of arms just to Iran alone. In the four years preceding 1973, such sales (through the Pentagon) reached a value of $1.28 billion. This in itself was no small figure, and must itself have had implications of no small importance, from the Soviet standpoint. But in the following four-year period (1973–1976) the volume of these sales was increased nearly ten times, to a total of $11 billion.

To get an idea of the effect of this upon the Russians, let us first recall than Iran is a border neighbor of the Soviet Union; and then let us imagine that the Soviet Union had first, in the early 1970s, inaugurated heavy arms sales to Mexico, and had then, in the middle of this decade, suddenly upped these sales by a factor of nearly 1000 percent and accompanied them, as we have actually done, by the dispatch of hundreds if not thousands of military technicians and advisors. Would the American government and public opinion have remained complacent and uninterested in the face of such behavior? And would we not have drawn our conclusions from it?

I have heard it argued: "Oh, well, they know we have no aggressive intentions. They know we would have no idea of using these arms for an attack on them." To this there are two things to be said.

When one attempts to explain to people in the Pentagon and to like-minded civilians that perhaps the Russians are not really eager to attack the West — that they have very good reasons for not planning or wishing to do anything of that sort, one is met with the reply: "Ah, yes, but look at the size of their armaments, and concede that in matters of this sort we cannot be bothered to take into account their intentions — intentions are too uncertain and too hard to determine; we can take into account only capabilities; we must assume the Russians to be desirous, that is, of doing anything bad to us that their capabilities would permit them to do." Now, is it really our view that *we* should take account only of their *capabilities*, disregarding their *intentions*, but that we should expect them to take account only of our supposed *intentions*, disregarding our *capabilities?* If it is, it may be said at once and with certainty that this, over the long term, will not wash. If we are going to disregard everything but their capabilities, we cannot simultaneously expect them to disregard everything but our intentions.

But secondly, when we agree over the course of four years to sell $11 billion worth of arms to the Iranians, we must remember that the question of intentions would not be, from the Soviet viewpoint, one that concerned us alone, or even us in the first instance. The Russians would have to ask themselves not what *we* would do with this enormous assemblage of weaponry but what the Iranians, in association with us or others, might do with it. And about this they will not be so easily reassured; for while it is true that the experiences of the Persians with their Russian neighbors over the course of the years have not always been pleasant ones, there have also been times when Persian behavior in this relationship left something to be desired from the Russian standpoint.

These sales to Iran are, of course, only part of the picture. Iran is not the only country in this region to have been receiving a massive infusion of American arms. During these same four years (1973–1976) Saudi Arabia has been permitted to purchase nearly $8 billion worth of them in the United States. And there are others as well.

It is simply unrealistic to suppose that the Russians would not be disquieted by this sudden outpouring of American arms to countries on or near their sensitive southern border, or that they do not feel compelled to draw their conclusions from it with relation to American aims in that part of the world. At best, this situation can be a source of serious confusion; at worst, it can be something more dangerous still.

Those who have sanctioned these massive sales of arms to the Moslem countries of the Near East defend the operation on the grounds that we have need to retain the good disposition of the more moderate of the Arab countries — that this, in fact, is a service to the Israelis insofar as it increases the influence of the moderate Arabs at the expense of the extremists.

In principle, there might be something to be said for this outlook. Of course, one should try to encourage the countries in question to take a helpful interest in a peaceful settlement of the Arab-Israeli question. But whether arms sales, and especially arms sales on this massive scale, are the best way to do this, is another thing. Such sales have, in the first place, ulterior effects, such as those we have just noted. There is also the fact that although one may know, as an arms supplier, into whose hands one delivers the arms, one can never be entirely sure in whose hands they are going to end up. Arms sometimes have longer lives than the individuals into whose hands they were initially entrusted. But beyond that, and taking the long view of the question, we have to recognize that the conflict engendered by the presence of the state of Israel in its present location is a conflict not just between Israel and her immediate neighbors but also, to one extent or another, between her and the entire Moslem community of that region. To which must be added the fact that arms, extravagantly given, have a way of wandering, sometimes, from one country to another. At a time when one is trying, by means of supplying Israel with arms, to keep that nation in a position where it can look after its own defense, does it really make sense to try to purchase the friendship of some of its Moslem neighbors by supplying them with even greater quantities of weaponry? Are there not more suitable ways of endeavoring to assure their support? Little gratitude or appreciation is to be earned, it seems to me, by great arms shipments of this nature, particularly when they come in the form of purchases, not gifts, and when the receiving country has such huge quantities of surplus money at its disposal that the cost of the weapons means little or nothing to it.

For all these reasons, the sooner these sales are curtailed, and eventually eliminated, the better. At best, this will take a long time; because orders have been placed and accepted; manufacturers have committed themselves; items are in the pipeline; and items already delivered will require spare parts if their value is to be retained. But it is none too soon to begin.

And this beginning is something we ought to undertake for our own reasons, unilaterally, without a quid pro quo from any other quarter. For this reason, it should not be made a factor in any negotiations we might conduct with the Russians over Near Eastern problems. It is a bad principle to attempt to get a price, in negotiation, for something you should do, and would do anyway, in your own interests; for if you do not get the price you want, then you are faced with the choice of backing down in the negotiations, or forfeiting the privilege of doing something you know it to be in your own interests to do. We may be sure that if the decision has been taken in Washington in all seriousness to terminate these ill-advised and potentially mischievous sales of arms to certain of the countries of the Near Eastern region, the effect, from the standpoint of the achievement of our own goals in the negotiations in question, cannot help but be positive.

There is one last point to be mentioned. When the Russians think of the problems of this area, they are obliged to think of them not just in connection with the issues I have mentioned but also with an eye to our military presence in Turkey, and perhaps even in regions farther afield. This might not be a topic of discussion in the talks themselves, but we could not expect it to be far from the Russian mind as those talks proceed. Turkey, after all, lies between the Soviet Union and much of the area we have here under discussion.

The question of the American military presence in Turkey, and that of NATO, will be treated below, in another connection. But it is desirable that anyone who thinks about possible Soviet-American exchanges of views concerning the problems of the Near East should have this question at least in the corner of his mind; for the Russians assuredly will have it in the corner of theirs, and their positions will not be fully intelligible to others unless this is recognized.

VI

East of Iran

Eastward from iran there stretches over several thousand miles, covering most of South and Southeast Asia and the Southeastern Pacific, a band of new, or relatively new, states: including Afghanistan, the countries of the Indian subcontinent, those of Southeast Asia, the Philippines, and Indonesia. Embracing fully a fourth of the world's inhabitants, this is obviously an immensely important portion of the earth's surface. Yet I am bound to say that I can see no vital interests of the United States anywhere in this region, and no reason why our involvement with any of the countries in question should go beyond that level of correct and disinterested relations, diplomatic and commercial, which was traditional to our dealings with distant countries before the madness of universal involvement overtook us in this postwar period. This does not preclude the activity of private American interests, cultural or commercial, to the extent this activity is welcome to the governments in question. It does not preclude a wide variety of cultural exchanges. It does not preclude efforts by our government to be helpful in special circumstances, such as disaster relief. It does not even preclude some developmental aid, although it is preferable that this be

[92]

extended through international channels rather than bilaterally. What it does preclude is political involvement, military aid, association as members of regional pacts, and efforts to bring pressure upon the respective governments with a view to changing the political systems or habits of the peoples in question. It implies, in other words, a relaxed, normal relationship, in which our government accepts responsibility for the correctness and generosity of its own behavior, but accepts no such responsibility for theirs, and takes an interest in their relations with third states only when, or if, these assume a character hostile to the United States.

So much for the general; now for the specific.

1. PAKISTAN

There are probably those who will argue that an exception be made for Pakistan, owing to our desire to retain military or quasi-military facilities there. This is a matter which concerns intimately our relations with the Soviet Union; and we shall have occasion to examine it more closely in that connection. Suffice it to say at this point that I find myself unable to believe that the necessity, or advantage, of the retention of these facilities is such as to override the obvious disadvantages. Their effect, to this point, has not only been to distort our relationship with Pakistan itself, causing us to behave, with relation to its government, in a way we would not have behaved in normal circumstances, but it has also interfered, and unfortunately so, with our relations with Pakistan's neighbors, notably India. It represents a distortion for purely military purposes, and questionable ones at that, of a pattern of relationships which could otherwise be made a clear, consistent, and irreproachable one.

2. INDIA

India, as just noted, is a country with which our relations have been unfavorably affected by our involvement with Pakistan. In addition to that, there has been some effect on American opinion, and to some extent on policy, of the authoritarian nature of the rule which Madame Gandhi thought it necessary to introduce. One of the factors has already disappeared. Let us hope the other will soon do likewise.

I am naturally aware of the special meaning that India has had for many Americans, and of the hopes that were so widely entertained, some years ago, that India might come to appear both as a close associate of the United States and as an inspiring example of the success of democratic institutions as the foundation for the development of a great country. Well, experience seems to have tempered the more sanguine expectations, on both sides. And perhaps this is not a bad thing. The moderate involvement of the Soviet Union in Indian affairs need be no great source of concern for us. It, too, like our own earlier involvement, will eventually find its own level. Perhaps an Indian-American relationship less burdened with heated expectations and sensitivities will produce, someday, opportunities for profitable collaboration greater than any now visible. We, in any case, can afford to wait.

3. SOUTHEAST ASIA

The same may be said, but with much greater emphasis, with relation to Southeast Asia. I find surprising the level of interest in the affairs of that area still manifested by portions of the American press and other media. Surely, if there are any peoples of which it may fairly be said that we have nothing to hope from them, it is the peoples of that unhappy region. Doubly surprising are the occasional suggestions that if relations could be established with the respective governments, then there might be a question of the resumption of U.S. aid in one form or another. When — oh, when — one asks, will we get over this curious fixation that a normal relationship of the United States with a smaller country implies aid from us to them? And where, again, in this particular instance, is our sense of dignity?

Our recent experiences in that part of the world — our effort, our miscalculations, our failure — are still fresh in everyone's mind. No one believed more strongly than I did, during the years in question, in the folly of the undertaking. We miscalculated in a number of respects. We found that the venture could not be carried to completion as we had conceived it. Very well. We took cognizance of our failure, pocketed our losses, and retired. It is for us now to come to terms, quietly, in our own minds and hearts, with the experience.

None of this vindicates the behavior of our recent opponents in Southeast Asia. Consistently, unscrupulously, and with passion, they misrepresented the motives and nature of our intervention in Vietnam, slandered our people, and exploited our discomfiture. Their own policies were clearly dominated by a driving lust for power, for which ideology and nationalism served as convenient disguises. The iron rule they have subsequently fastened on the peoples who fell under their power is many times worse, from the political standpoint and that of human freedom, than anything we ever tried to bring to those same peoples. Once again, as in the case of Cuba, it may well be that eventually (not soon) they will succeed in creating their own version of a pseudo-Marxist civilization, which will indeed eliminate certain of the seamier aspects of life that thrived in those countries before and during the period of our involvement, will produce a certain floor in living standards beneath which the common people cannot fall, and will afford to those people, if not political freedom, then such satisfactions as a puritanical egalitarianism and the absence of any conspicuous foreign presence may afford.

So what? Let others argue as to whether this is or is not preferable to the quite different conditions which we, in our American provincialism and naïveté, once dreamed of bringing to these peoples. We have no need to strike judgments about this. Least of all do we need to engage our responsibility in any way in the further affairs of the region. There is no reason why we should be in a hurry to conclude relations of any kind with the respective governments or to manifest any particular interest in what they are doing. They won. We lost. It is now their show. Let us be content if the period that ensues before we find it necessary to have anything more to do with them is a good long one. And if, in the meantime, either the Chinese or the Russians dabble in their affairs, our attitude should be: you are heartily welcome to each other; it serves you both right.

4. THE PHILIPPINES

Our involvement with the Philippines over these past eighty years has been a close and tangled one. It is not my purpose here to depict our conduct in this relationship as a triumph of consistent liberality and enlightenment. I am sure it would be possible to point to many turnings at which we did the wrong thing. We did, of course, liberate them from the Spaniards. Perhaps, in the light of history, this was all wrong. Perhaps we should have left them to their fate: presumably to be similarly "liberated" at some point by the British or the Germans or the Japanese. Perhaps that would have been more virtuous. In any case, we tried hard, in the decades that followed, to give them a decent interim rule, some degree of economic and political development, and, in time, an open road to independence. We did not wait for the anticolonial pressures of the post–World War II period before offering them independence at the end of a reasonable transition period; and when the period was up, we actually made good on the commitment. It might be alleged, I suppose, that we were responsible for involving them in the war with Japan in the first place. But it was also we who liberated them, at very considerable cost in American lives and substance, from the Japanese. And in the thirty-odd years of their independence we have showered them with every conceivable sort of developmental and financial aid.

If, at the end of this long and tangled story, there remains any sort of moral balance in our favor, the Philippine leaders, it seems to me, have not shown any particular awareness of it. Nor has the degree of stability in their internal affairs afforded much grounds for supposing that a continuation of this sort of interest on our part would be a rewarding exercise either from our standpoint or from that of the Philippine people as a whole. Those Americans, in particular, who saw the main objective of our involvement there in the development of democratic institutions on the islands can find little encouragement at the end of thirty years of their independence.

We did, of course, keep in the Philippines, in the wake of World War II, a number of bases for our armed forces. It was not our understanding, initially, that this practice was objectionable from the standpoint of the Philippine government; and indeed, it was given a form of regional, as well as Philippine, sanction in the form of the conclusion of the Southeast Asia Treaty Organization (SEATO) in 1954.

Some of the bases were withdrawn, progressively, over the course of the intervening years. Two, however — the Clark Air Force Base and the Subic Bay Naval Base — remain.

The original justification for the maintenance of these two bases has now been extensively undermined. Our involvement in Southeast Asia has been liquidated. Communist China is no longer regarded as an enemy. Our military presence on the island of Taiwan is also in process of liquidation, and the process is nearly complete. SEATO itself has ceased to exist.

In the light of these circumstances, President Marcos, who now finds himself in a somewhat different international situation than that which prevailed some years ago, has called, repeatedly and — as it seems to me — not too politely, for our relinquishment of the two remaining bases. And when we indicated reluctance (I cannot quite see why) to relinquish them, he demanded in effect that we pay a tribute of at least a billion dollars for the privilege of continuing to maintain them there.

As already indicated, I can see no reason at all to pay any tribute of this nature, whether it is a billion dollars or any other sum; nor can I see any reason why the bases should not be removed at once. Even if our naval and military interests in the region were still of such a nature as to suggest a serious need for them (which they do not appear to be), it would be highly unsound, politically and psychologically, to get into the habit of paying this sort of financial price (which would surely rise with the years) for the privilege of retaining them. The original theory was that they contributed to the defense of the Philippines as well as that of ourselves and the general peace of the region. If the Filipinos no longer see it that way, this in itself would remove a good part of the justification for their retention.

The position of retaining on the territory of a smaller state military facilities which the government of that smaller state does not want there, and paying huge annual bribes as a form of hush money to keep the leaders of that state quiet and to cause them to accommodate themselves reluctantly, and for the moment, to this practice, is not a position in which the United States should ever choose to appear. The American response to the situation that now exists should be, surely, the immediate, complete, resolute, and wordless withdrawal of the facilities and the equipment they contain, leaving to the Philippine government the real estate, and only that. We can find a very useful precedent for what needs to be done in recalling the prompt and incisive manner in which General de Gaulle caused the

French to remove themselves from a number of France's African colonies when the latter demanded their independence. The consequences were in no way disastrous. On the contrary, France's relations with certain of these states in the ensuing years have been among the happiest of those enjoyed by any former colonial European power with its erstwhile colonies. It is high time that we, too, put an end to our practice of letting other people have it both ways.

VII

The Far East

1. CHINA

If Southeast Asia need no longer concern us, as I fervently
hope it will not, then it is time to move to the countries that lie to
the north of it. Of these the first, of course, is China.

We find that great country, so soon after the death of Mao, once
again in a delicate state of internal transition. The outcome of this
process need not greatly concern us; but it may usefully serve as a
reminder to us of the danger of building too extensively, in our
foreign relations, on individual personalities at the head of a foreign
state. These come and go; the state remains. When it comes to lay-
ing out American policies designed to stand the test of time, it is better to look at the long-term interests, and the long-term behavior, of
a state than at the personalities who momentarily head it. This does
not mean that personalities can be ignored, particularly the great and
dominant ones, to which category Mao obviously belonged. It does
mean that one should not place too much reliance on personalities
when and if their policies deviate radically from what seems to be
the natural and traditional manner of behavior of the state in question.

China has been going through what is, for it, an epoch-making up-heaval in its national life. It has not finished going through it. This upheaval will leave its marks on Chinese society; we must not, in fact, expect that society ever to be entirely what it was before the ad-vent of Mao. Yet in most respects the Chinese people must be ex-pected to continue to be what they have been in the past: a great people, immensely intelligent, greatly talented as the creators and bearers of a civilization, but very different from ourselves, out-wardly polite and ceremonious (to a point) but inwardly prickly in their relations with foreigners, not a people to lend themselves easily to any intimacy with non-Chinese, and particularly with non-Orien-tals. We should not be misled by a certain facility in communication with foreigners which distinguishes the Chinese very markedly from their Japanese neighbors. This may appear to ease the process of un-derstanding. More often it masks differences all the more profound because they so seldom rise to the surface of frank expostulation.

Americans now have a history of more than a century of contact and involvement with the Chinese. The record of it is not very cred-itable to us. Motives of commercial or personal gain have too often been mixed with those of professed religious or political altruism. The attitudes of Americans who have had to do extensively with the Chinese have varied between an extreme and unwarranted cynicism and a patronizing sentimentalization. Many of those who resided there permitted themselves to be subtly corrupted by the various amenities of a foreigner's life in a Chinese milieu; and the Chinese showed themselves (for which they cannot be blamed) highly adept at promoting this corruption and taking advantage of it in delicate ways. There were always notable exceptions, of course; but by and large it may be said that the contacts between individual Americans and the Chinese in earlier decades, before Mao, showed neither side off at its best, and did no one much good. One of the constructive features of the Mao period, as I see it, was to remove this body of American expatriates from Chinese society and to get our relations back to where, in the circumstances, they best belong: to the exchanges, that is, between responsible representatives of governments. If person-to-person contacts between Americans and Chinese are ever to be resumed on any extensive scale, and particularly ones that involve the prolonged residence of any number of Americans in China, they should, strange as this may sound to American ears, be carefully designed and closely controlled.

Our relations with the present Chinese regime are a familiar story, which there is no need to recount. At the heart of the difficulty lies, in the eyes of many of our people, the fact that this is a regime dedicated, in its own curious way, to Communist principles and highly distrustful of our own. But more important than the ideological differences (which, as we have seen in the case of Russia, do not alone preclude either peaceful coexistence or normal official relations) has been the purely traditional and nationalistic bone of contention arising from the American relationship to the regime on the island of Taiwan.

The United States leaders, in the period 1943–1948, committed two dreadful errors in this direction. The first was the promise to Chiang Kai-shek, at the Cairo Conference in late 1943, that we would support the return of Taiwan to China — and this, before we had had any chance either to consult with other interested powers or to test the wishes of the inhabitants. (Perhaps some of those who are anxious to get at the psychological roots of American reactions affecting foreign policy would like to examine why it is that one hears the demand for "majority rule" so often raised with respect to Southern Africa and other regions, but almost never with respect to Formosa.) The second was to permit the Chiang regime, at that time a failing competitor for supreme power on the mainland, to move out to the island and to establish itself there with the claim, recognized by ourselves, to be the government of all of China. On the consequences of these mistakes we have been strung up, in our relations with Peking, ever since.

These two mistakes were intimately interconnected; and this makes it doubly difficult to undo them today. Theoretically we could, years ago — before establishing relations with the present Peking regime — have declared ourselves in favor of self-determination for the inhabitants of the island, demanding that they be given some sort of a plebiscitary choice between the three conceivable possibilities: independence, continued association with Japan, or re-incorporation into China. But this would have meant both undermining the claim of the Chiang government to be ruling from Formosa-Taiwan as the legitimate government of China, and reneging on our own expressed commitment, of 1943, to the thesis that the island was a proper part of China. We could, conversely, have withdrawn our recognition of the Chiang regime as the legitimate government of all of China; but this would have meant that we challenged the correctness of its position and its activity on Taiwan, and we would have been in logic bound to see the island returned to whatever *was*, if not Chiang, the legitimate government of China. We got ourselves, in short, into a situation of great confusion; and we are still in it today.

The action of Messrs. Nixon and Kissinger in establishing de facto relations with the Peking regime was in itself a constructive one, although it would have been even more so if it had been carried out in a normal and businesslike manner and without the histrionics of the Nixon visit to Peking. There is no reason not to have de facto relations, or even (depending on circumstances) de jure ones, with a Communist regime, if useful practical purposes can be served thereby. Only the combined tactical genius of Mr. Kissinger and Chou En-lai, one must admit, could have found a way of reconciling this, in practice if not in theory, with our continued de jure recognition of the regime on Taiwan. But this tour de force was bound to be of limited duration. The situation resulting from it was never one intended or expected to last indefinitely. Now Chinese patience, in Peking at least, is beginning to wear thin. Something more, presumably, will soon have to be done.

It is probably too late to return to anything like a demand for self-determination for the Taiwanese. This, strongly as it would accord with traditional American policy, would now be disruptive of our relations with *both* regimes. A total abandonment of the Nationalist regime, on the other hand, is also unthinkable. The island, under its authority, has done too well in its quasi-independent status, and has developed a form of life and of economy too different from that of the mainland, to be suddenly sacrificed in this way. Eventually, one must expect, the Chinese being what they are, that the Nationalist regime, which is not lacking in a certain bargaining power vis-à-vis the mainland, will contrive to come to some sort of compromise which will give the island a semi-autonomous status in exchange for its own abandonment of the claim to be the government of all of China. It should be our concern to do nothing to impede such a settlement.

Our present positive possibilities limit themselves to two. First, we could reduce our representation on the island of Taiwan to a de facto status. There are precedents for that in the recent actions of other powers. This, we should probably do, as soon and as gracefully as we can, making it clear that this change would also imply the automatic voidance of the defense treaty with the Taiwan regime, to the provisions of which we are still theoretically committed. This is something that no American will do with a light heart; for it does seem a shabby way to treat a government with which one has long had good relations; but it is a step that will surely have to be taken at some point, and it will probably be easier for a new administration to take it in the earlier stages of its incumbency, when it is not yet extensively involved personally with the regime in question, than later, when closer personal ties have been established.

To take this move will unquestionably ease our relations with Peking. But it will leave us faced with the second question, which is: whether then, immediately, to raise our representation in Peking to full de jure status. This is recommended by some very knowledgeable people. It, too, is something that must be expected to occur sooner or later. It might, however, be argued that we should, out of respect for the regime on Taiwan, delay this step until some accept-

able accommodation has been reached between the two rival regimes. It could well be argued that this even-handed approach
would close fewer doors and leave us greater latitude of decision
towards the problem as a whole.

I doubt that any outsider can see clearly all aspects of this highly
delicate question, and I can go no further in the way of comment on
it. It might be well, in any case, to consult with the Japanese before
proceeding further in the search for the right solution, for although
they have committed themselves, clearly and unequivocably, to the
Peking position, their views might be enlightening.

If and when this question of our relations with Taiwan has finally
been settled in a manner acceptable to Peking, and our relations with
Communist China have thus been formally normalized, we will be
faced with the shaping of our long-term relations with the latter.
This will happen naturally, in the treatment of a multitude of day-
by-day practical problems. There is no visible reason why we should
feel it necessary to draw wide general conclusions at any early date.
But two or three comments are perhaps in order.

First, let us be very careful not to try to push this relationship too
far and too fast. It is a delicate one, with many possibilities for fric-
tion and misunderstanding. Let us be mindful at all times of the
great differences in experience, in outlook, and in mentality (not to
mention those of sheer national interest) that divide us from the
Chinese, and be careful, accordingly, not to press us both into dealings or involvements that could easily mean one thing to them and
another to us. With people who are very different from oneself, a
polite, respectful, but slightly distant and formal relationship is
sometimes better, and presents fewer dangers, than effusive attempts
to chumminess. The Chinese will, in many respects, have reservations about us. Let us also have a few about them, at least until we
are entirely sure of our ground.

There are, I know, those who have dreams of a far more intimate
and highly political association with the Chinese. They have

dreams — strangely old-fashioned dreams, right out of earlier decades — of the Chinese as our great friends and partners, not just in Far Eastern affairs but in world affairs generally. They would like to see us move to realize these dreams without delay.

I am unable to see the foundation for such a view. China occupies a wholly different position, geographically and historically, in world affairs than our own. She has her own set of national interests, which are quite different from ours. The respective interests are not extensively in conflict, except occasionally with regard to activities in the Third World. But they are also far from identical. Let us collaborate where we can, agree to differ where we cannot, and see whether we cannot contrive to live reasonably peaceably together for the time being, despite our differences, not asking too much of each other — or too little.

More serious — indeed, a real aberration of American thinking about the future of our relations with China — is the view that we should "tilt" our relations with China against the Soviet Union — should try, in other words, to make use of China as an instrument for the advancement of our interests, and the reduction of Soviet ones, in the Soviet-American relationship. I find it difficult to say how strongly I disapprove of any such suggestion. It assumes a greater basic identity of our long-term interests with China than with Russia — something which is in no way proven. It would involve us in the Soviet-Chinese conflict, the issues of which have nothing to do with our own interests. It would add an unnecessary burden to our relations with the Soviet Union, and would leave us in a weakened position if the two great Communist powers should arrive at some sort of composition of their differences — something they would do without the slightest regard for us, if it suited their interests.

But worst of all, for us to engage ourselves on one side or the other in this conflict would bring us close to something that should be, if anything should, a basic principle of American foreign policy: namely, that bad relations with a third state should never, but really

never, be, for another government, the price of America's friendship; nor should that friendship ever be extended as a species of
reward or encouragement for such bad relations. The world has
troubles enough without our going out of our way to increase them.
If we are going to proceed from the recognition that war and conflict
between great powers in the modern age have never produced happy
results, we must not ignore that lesson in the present instance. It can
be argued, of course, but only from the most simplistic and militaristic of views (only from a view that sees war between the Soviet
Union and the United States as virtually inevitable) that the
Chinese-Soviet conflict has benefited the West in its conflict with the
Soviet Union. If so, it is a cheap and ephemeral victory. The Western community must find other, more solid and more positive ways
than this of improving its relationship to the Soviet Union than by
trying to play China off against it, if the catastrophe we all fear is to
be averted and if the great constructive possibilities of the Soviet-
American relationship are ultimately to be realized.

2. JAPAN

There can be no question but that the cornerstone of American policy in the Far East should be Japan.

There are several reasons for this. One of them is geographic —
geo-political, if you will. Japan bears a relation to the mainland of
Asia similar to that of the British Isles to the mainland of Europe.
Like Britain, and like ourselves, Japan is a great overseas and trading
power. It shares, in this respect, many of our own interests. Like
ourselves, it is concerned to see a reasonable balance of power preserved on the Asiatic mainland. It is taking care not to involve itself
in the conflict between the two great Communist powers of the
mainland, and is concerned, as we should be, to do what it can to
prevent that conflict's taking military form. It shares the concern for

the security of the Northern Pacific Ocean which is our greatest strategic interest in that area.

Japan, furthermore, is *the* great industrial workshop of the Far East. Nothing else now in existence there compares with it. It is the only place where all the sinews of modern armed strength, from the most elementary to the most sophisticated, can be produced, if necessary, on short order. Should this potential come under the control of, or into close association with, one of the two great Communist landpowers, there is no predicting what uses might be made of it, and no certainty at all that these would be ones conducive to our security. So long as there prevails a relationship of mutual confidence, of community of aims, and of loyal collaboration between the Japanese and ourselves, we can be sure that this great hive of industrial and commercial activity will be a force for peace. Left to themselves, the Japanese, to avoid total isolation, would have to give a wholly different value to their relations with their great mainland neighbors; and we could never be sure where these new relationships would find their ending. Japan's industrial power, in other words, is so tremendous a factor in world affairs that it can hardly help constituting a force either for great good or for great bad. So long as we have a close and solid relationship with the Japanese, we can hope to prevent it from becoming the latter. If we lose that relationship, we cannot tell.

All this is important; but it is not the most important thing. The most important thing is something else, which is very hard to describe: and that is the curious sort of moral obligation, and of moral opportunity, which we have before us in our relations with the Japanese. They, too, are a remarkable people: highly intelligent, immensely industrious, sensitive, thoughtful, often even brooding, as inept at communication as the Chinese are facile, but not so self-centered as the Chinese, more interested than are the Chinese in what lies around them in the world, including ourselves, and endowed (at least in their finest elements) with a tremendous, tragic, sometimes even noble earnestness of conscience and obligation. Like the Chinese, they are very different people from ourselves; and if the recent War of the Pacific had not intervened, I would have been tempted to say, as I have just said in the case of China: let us not push an unnatural intimacy too far and too fast. But the war did intervene. We were, as a result of it, thrown into contact with the Japanese in the closest way in the post-hostilities period. And out of this there did come a species of intimacy — an intimacy born of conflict and much agony, particularly on the Japanese side, but an intimacy, nevertheless. We learned a great deal about each other, good and bad, in those unhappy years. That is the nature of all intimacies.

I am not speaking here of anything sentimental. I am not speaking of love or admiration. Such things, often as they may be invoked in the effusions of romantic nationalists and wartime propagandists, have no place in the real lives of nations. I am speaking of something much deeper: a common recognition that fate — or, if you will, the mistakes of earlier generations — have thrown us in each other's path; that the effort to work things out in opposition to each other has proven worse than useless; that we have no choice but to contrive to do it together.

The responsibility lies most heavily on us Americans; for it was we who defeated the Japanese; we who asked, through the formula of unconditional surrender, for a total power (and thus a total responsibility) over their affairs; we who somewhat brashly undertook to show them how to live, in this modern age, more happily, more safely, and more usefully, than they had lived before. You could hardly assume a greater responsibility than this. But they, too, are not without responsibility. They have to do, here, in the person of the United States, with an ally somewhat humbled by intervening events. Experience has now shown to many Americans the dangers of overweening ambitions and of exaggerated self-glorification. We are, as a result, less impressive to others than we used to be, and less confident that we have the answers. We, too, then, need help and guidance. And we need careful handling by our friends. The Japanese have come by their knowledge of us in painful ways. But they know us, as a result, very well indeed — better perhaps than most of our international associates. Their potential influence upon us is not to be underrated. This, too, is a responsibility.

What all this adds up to is that we have here a relationship which, precisely because it was born in pain and conflict, is unique as a test of the ability of both parties to handle themselves wisely and usefully in international affairs. If we cannot make a success of this, we are in a bad way, generally.

It is for all these reasons that Japan must continue to be, as she has been since the recent war, the cornerstone of our position in the Far East — but not a passive cornerstone — rather, an active one, a talking one — a stone which often harbors a superior wisdom — a stone to be consulted, in some instances to be looked to for guidance, to be looked to sometimes even for leadership.

The action of President Nixon in suddenly visiting Peking and establishing de facto relations with the Chinese Communist regime, in 1972, and this without advance consultation with, or warning to, the Japanese, came as a great shock to the latter. Polite, as always, they concealed their feelings to some extent publicly, moved promptly to establish full diplomatic relations with Peking on their own (which implied their independent embarkation, for the first time since 1945, on a major diplomatic course, and thus a certain distancing from us), then resumed outwardly normal and cordial relations with the U.S. government, even to the point of permitting the visit of Emperor Hirohito to Washington. We would be wrong, however, if we allowed this last circumstance to persuade us that they had forgotten the experience of 1972, and that the inroads this had made in their confidence in us had been entirely eradicated.

The change of administrations in Washington provides the most suitable possible time for a serious effort to reassure the Japanese as to the loyalty and consideration they may expect at our hands over the coming period. For this, it is of outstanding importance that our representation in Tokyo should be in the hands of persons well qualified by experience and interest to understand what is going on in the Japanese mind and to explain our policies to them in a way they can understand. If this is done, it is not too much to hope that the relationship can be placed on such a footing that it will bear the required weight as the cornerstone of our position in East Asia.

3. KOREA

Korea represents one of the two most explosive and dangerous spots on our political map of the world, the other one being the Near East. The circumstances of our military intervention there in 1950 and of our subsequent military involvement with the South Korean regime are fresh in everyone's mind. They may, however, be misleading as guides to the future. Our action in 1950 was taken against a background of high instability throughout the Far East in the wake of the Pacific war and the extension of Chinese Communist rule to all of mainland China. There was much uncertainty. Imaginations were inflamed. The repercussions of an unopposed seizure by the North Korean Communists of the southern half of the Korean peninsula, where we, after all, had taken the Japanese surrender and for which — in the absence of a peace treaty with Japan — we had a special responsibility, could easily have sent ripples throughout the Far East, and not least to Japan, which could have led to a Communist seizure of power there, too, and thus have deprived our recent military victory there of most of its meaning. To which must be added the recollection that the reins of power in Moscow were then in the hands of Joseph Stalin, and the attitude towards us of the regime then in power in Peking was hostile in the extreme. In these circumstances, the decision to intervene in Korea was a sound one (although it would have been better to restrict our objectives to the restoration of the *status quo ante* and not to attempt the advance to the Yalu).

Today, circumstances are quite different. There is a fully independent and stable Japanese government. The same is true for Taiwan. Power in Moscow is in the hands of people who, whatever one thinks of them, represent a great change from the Soviet regime of Stalin's last years. It is doubtful that either Moscow or Peking wants to see at this juncture the sort of crisis that would be introduced by a renewal of the civil war in Korea.

To this must be added a very unhappy and disturbing factor: namely, the nature and behavior of the Park regime in South Korea: its apparent inability, or unwillingness, to maintain its rule there by any other than the most brutal methods of repression; and the cynicism and lack of respect for our own country that it has shown by its dabbling in American domestic politics and its attempts to bend American legislators to its own uses. Not only does this pattern of behavior throw into question the soundness of our relationship with that regime, per se, but it threatens to undermine, over the long term, the stability of South Korea, to hasten the very crisis we all would like to avoid, and to involve us, in this way, in a confusing and dangerous situation.

There has been much to be said, in recent years, both for and against the continued stationing of American forces in South Korea. For long, a good case could be made out either way. Recent events have, however, to my mind and to that of many others, tipped the scales in favor of withdrawal. This does not mean abrupt withdrawal, or even withdrawal in the absence of careful consultation with those others whose interests are intimately involved. The Japanese should certainly be carefully and attentively consulted before any decisions are taken at all. They have a vital interest in the situation on the Korean peninsula. It means more to them than it does to us. But it would also be well to keep in touch, in this connection, with both Peking and Moscow. Both of those powers have, as noted above, an interest in seeing to it that the situation in Korea develops peacefully and does not provoke unnecessary crises and troubles in the surrounding region. It is not to be excluded that if we effect our withdrawal in a manner reasonably acceptable, and for reasons well explained and comprehensible, to both of those powers, their influence may be helpful in seeing to it that the change is effected peacefully and without disturbance to the stability of the region.

VIII

======

NATO

We come now to the most extensive, the most long-standing, and the most intimate of America's overseas commitments: those that flow from the North Atlantic Pact and the Organization set up to promote its purposes. Here, it will be best to start with the most questionable aspect of this commitment: that which affects the tattered southeastern fringe of the alliance — Greece and Turkey.

1. Greece and Turkey

Many years ago, when the Atlantic Alliance was concluded, I stood alone, I believe, among those who had to do with its conclusion, in opposing the inclusion of Greece and Turkey among its members. I did this not from any sense of antagonism or lack of sympathy towards those two countries but from the recognition that their interests were ones which in many respects departed very far from those that were central to NATO as a whole, and from the fear that their inclusion would lead to pressures on NATO to involve itself in questions having little or nothing to do with its stated purposes. By no stretch of the imagination could the two countries be regarded as *Atlantic* powers. The roots of democracy, in Turkey above all, were not profound. Indeed, the only visible grounds for including them was to enlist them in a general coalition against Russia (which was not NATO's original purpose) and to make use of their territory for military purposes aimed against the Soviet Union. It was a part, in short, of the extreme militarization of thinking about the Cold War which overcame so many of us under the shock of the Korean War.

A quarter of a century has now passed; and certain of the apprehensions which I then entertained have now unfortunately taken on flesh and blood. In the course of the last two or three years the governments of both countries have made it evident that the differences between them mean more to them than any of the considerations that are supposed to underlie their association with NATO. Mr. Caramanlis inaugurated his return to power, in 1974, with an announcement of Greece's withdrawal from all association with NATO in the military field, gave formal notice, as a starter, of Greece's withdrawal from the NATO Defense Planning Committee, and called publicly for a three-year phasing out of NATO bases on Greek territory. The Turks, in the ensuing winter, refused to participate in NATO exercises on the grounds that the Greeks had refused permission for flights over the Aegean. Plainly, the NATO presence in the Aegean–Black Sea region was already at that time in a state of serious disarray.

Even more unpleasant have been the attitudes taken by both governments towards the United States. The Caramanlis government showed extreme irritation with the United States over the latter's failure to support its own cause against that of the previous regime, holding us to blame for the long endurance in power of the colonels. (This criticism implied that the United States ought to be involved in Greek internal-political affairs, but on Mr. Caramanlis's side — not the other.) Mr. Caramanlis's assumption of power was then followed by a veritable orgy of anti-American demonstrations — demonstrations which obviously enjoyed the government's sympathic tolerance if not its inspiration. Both countries then did their best to involve us and use us to their particular ends in their squabble over Cyprus. And in mid-1975 the Turks, out of spite for the action of our Congress in banning further aid to Turkey (which had obviously come to be taken by them as a right rather than a privilege), announced that, the U.S.-Turkish defense agreements having lost their validity, the activities of all the American military installations in Turkey would be suspended, and the installations themselves placed under the supervision of the Turkish armed forces.

In the end, new agreements were sketched out with both countries (in March and April 1976), envisaging continuation of the activity of most of the bases for a further four-year period, but under command of the respective governments and only in return for sizable financial tributes from the United States government: $1.6 billion, allegedly, of aid to Turkey (of which $1 billion was to be military) for the four-year period, and $700 million, similarly, to the Greeks. Several of the installations in question having been concerned extensively with intelligence-gathering, it was also provided that any intelligence gained in this way should now be shared with the host country.

Both of these agreements were subject to approval by Congress. At the time of writing, this approval had not yet been forthcoming. (The agreement with the Greek government was, I believe, only in the nature of a "statement of intentions.")

I can see nothing to be said for the final approval of these agreements, and hope that the new administration will not encourage their ratification. They involve, in the first place, the same principle as that which we noted in connection with the bases in the Philippines. When one has to bribe allies to induce them to permit the retention of American facilities on their territory, this is already evidence that the relationship is an unsound one, and the ally in question not fully reliable. Beyond that, each of these agreements serves as a precedent for others. We may be sure that if these particular agreements are ratified, no one — from now on — will think of accepting American military installations on his territory, no matter how helpful these may be to his own defense, without demanding the highest price he thinks he can get for what we are supposed to see as an act of graciousness on his part. The insistence on the bases' being put under the "command" or "supervision" of the respective government resembles the demand for the reassertion of the Panamanian government's theoretical sovereign control over the canal, and is, like the arrangement the Panamanians are demanding, pregnant with possibilities for embarrassment, confusion, and humiliation of the American forces involved.

There would not appear to be much to be lost by the abandonment of these facilities. The NATO military arrangements affecting that region are already, as we have just noted, in extensive disarray. And any sensitive military intelligence shared with the Greek and Turkish governments would lose, for obvious reasons, a great part of its value.

Finally, in these days of anxious discussion over problems of government spending, budget balancing, and tax reduction, a layman would think that the prospect of saving $2.3 billion would not be an insignificant item in our calculations. Indeed, the assumption that such a sum means little or nothing to us when military matters are involved — an assumption reflected in the obvious ease with which we acquiesced to the respective demands — only stands as a further example of the double standard in the evaluating of money of which I spoke in connection with the military-industrial complex. It is evidently not easy for us to accustom ourselves to the realization that at this juncture in world affairs the only people who can afford to sling such sums of money carelessly around are the Arabs. We no longer belong in that category.

All in all, then, I wonder whether it might not be better, in these circumstances, to let the bases be phased out, as the Greeks and Turks have themselves been demanding, leaving to our Western European NATO allies the responsibility for designing the future shape of the relationship of these two countries to NATO. This would not preclude American support for whatever arrangements the rest of them might arrive at. It would not even preclude the stationing of American personnel at NATO installations in the region, under NATO command, if the host countries had nothing against it. There is a precedent for this in the form of the Incirlik NATO base in Turkey, which the Turks did not include in their general crackdown on the American bases, although some three thousand Americans, it would appear, were at that time still serving there. The difference would only be that we would no longer deal directly with the Greeks and the Turks on these matters; that would be left to the Western European NATO partners, to whose initiative we would look for deciding what degree of NATO's involvement with the two governments in question would be most compatible with the interests of the Alliance as a whole. It is, after all, their security, rather than our own, which is primarily at stake in the solution to this problem.

It is not to be supposed that such an arrangement would be in any way objectionable to the Greek government. One of the first things Mr. Caramanlis did, amid the anti-American effusions of his first weeks in power, was to pay a demonstrative visit to France. This was very suitable, for France was a country to which he now had a special link in their common repudiation of a military association with NATO. An orientation of the Greeks towards France as their principal Western military connection, rather than towards the United States, strikes me as a splendid idea. Perhaps it would even ease the task of the other NATO partners in finding a proper place for Greece in relationship to the Alliance.

A withdrawal of the bases in Greece and Turkey would have the added advantage of making it easier for us to avoid involvement in the Cyprus question. We have no reason to take sides or to be maneuvered into any sort of responsibility with relation to this dispute. The Turks, so far as I am aware, did not consult us before taking their recent action (although they did not hesitate to use weapons we had placed in their hands for a wholly different purpose). The Greek-Cypriote regime in the other part of the island has lagged behind no other in the tolerance it has shown towards anti-American demonstrations among the populace. It showed no haste in finding, much less punishing, the individuals who murdered the American ambassador there, Mr. Rodger P. Davies, in 1974. We have wisely refrained, to date, from replacing the murdered envoy; and there is not the faintest reason for hastening to do so.

Two more problems present themselves in this connection: that of our naval presence in the Mediterranean, and our supply lines to Israel in that region. As to the naval presence I shall have one or two things to say in connection with our relations with the Soviet Union. As far as the supply line is concerned: our ability to use Greek facilities under some new agreement would rest, in any case, on the momentary benevolence of the Greek government, which we are obliged to view as an uncertain quantity, at best. The undermining of our position in that body of water may in truth be already a matter of fact rather than of choice. The dangers such a situation presents can presumably be mitigated by the timely stockpiling of supplies in Israel in the periods between crises. Beyond that, this vulnerability will simply have to be accepted, as one of the facts of life; and we and the Israelis — primarily the latter, secondarily ourselves — will have to accommodate ourselves to it as best we can.

2. ITALY

Moving westward from the troubles and tensions of the Aegean, we come to another of NATO's greatest problems: the condition of Italy — not only the chaotic and precarious state of government in that country but also the growing political prominence and involvement of the Italian Communist Party. This last, in particular, has been a source of much anxiety to large parts of the American public, including certain highly placed figures of the last administration.

The uneasiness is not misplaced. The Italian Communists already command roughly a third of the votes of the Italian electorate, and are very close to preempting the place of the Christian Socialists as Italy's strongest party. They could presumably at any time, if they wished, enter the government as the leading member of a coalition — either with the Christian Socialists or with the Socialists. They already participate prominently in the governing of several of Italy's greatest cities. Their ideological inroads on the Catholic hierarchy and laity have also not been insignificant.

The possible dangers of a Communist participation in the government of Italy are often seen as lying primarily in the advantages this would give to the Soviet Union for interference in, and even domination of, Italian political life. Actually, this is the lesser of the dangers that are to be feared. The Italian Communist Party has already emancipated itself very extensively from Soviet ideological and organizational control, and would be even more independent if it were to come into a share in the governmental power in Italy. The rank and file are for the most part not Communists at all in Moscow's terms. The revolutionary tradition with which they are associated is not at all that of Russia. They know next to nothing of Russian communism. The discipline of political responsibility would move them even farther from it. The leaders are, to be sure, firm intellectual Marxists, but primarily of the Western variety, not the Eastern. Were they to advance to a monopoly of political power in Italy, as they might well do once admitted to participation in a coalition, the shape they would try to give to Italian society would probably resemble that of Tito's Yugoslavia more than that of Russia. This would be not at all to the liking of the Moscow leaders. Nor would the assumption of formal political responsibility by the Communists in Italy, even as members of a coalition, be agreeable to Moscow from the standpoint of the repercussions it would have in

Eastern Europe; for the example of yet another Communist party in power (after those of Yugoslavia and China) going its own way and developing its own brand of communism in defiance of Moscow would unquestionably influence the Eastern European Communist leaders and be exploited by them as a means of winning greater independence from Russian tutelage for themselves. It is for these reasons, no doubt, that the Kremlin has already shown itself opposed to the advancement to power of any of the Western European Communist parties, the Italian above all, by democratic rather than revolutionary means.

The danger of such a development, from the standpoint of the United States and the other major NATO powers, lies not so much, then, in the possibility that the Soviet leadership might take advantage of it as in the way in which it would affect Italy's position in NATO and her relations with the other members of the European Community. The fact that the Italian Communist Party no longer opposes Italy's continued membership in NATO does not significantly change the nature of this problem. It would be out of the question, in such a contingency, that Italy should continue to participate in any of the NATO bodies or activities where sensitive information is involved or where the observance of a high degree of security is essential. (Actually, it would seem to me most unlikely even in present conditions, given the state of the Italian government and the degree of involvement of the Italian Communist Party in political life, that information coming into the hands of the Italian government through participation in NATO could be adequately protected.)

This means that a participation of the Italian Communist Party in government would have, at best, the effect of placing Italy in a position similar to that of France and Greece: unwilling or unqualified, that is, to take part in the military activities of the Alliance. But this in turn would mean that the entire southern tier of the NATO community had become in effect unsuited for participation in the military side of NATO's activity; for Portugal has not yet achieved a

degree of stability which would permit a wholly normal participation, and even if Spain were to be admitted, as some would like,
the instability bound to mark its political life for some time into the
future would similarly militate against its full-fledged association
with the military activities of the organization.

Now, France has already separated herself from NATO in the military sense and Greece and Turkey have virtually done so. If the
same were to occur in the case of the Italians, NATO would be
reduced in effect to its Northern European core — Britain, Benelux,
Western Germany, and (but also not without certain limitations)
Denmark and Norway, plus of course Canada and the United
States. (For purposes of this discussion one need not include Iceland,
which has no armed forces.) For the others, membership would
primarily be of a symbolic or honorary character: a mode of affirma-
tion of respect for Western cultural and political values, and the formal documenting of an unwillingness to drift into any of the Communist camps or into that of the "non-aligned."

Actually, this would not necessarily be as unfortunate as it may
initially sound. It would leave the Alliance intact in its strongest
parts, with much greater compactness and greater facility of decision. Its paper strength would be diminished; its real strength —
little, if at all.

If the general thrust of my argument is, as the reader will by this
time have noted, the advocacy of a pruning of unnecessary or
marginal involvements and the paring down of America's commitments to a point where she can better cope with the important ones,
then the same principle could, I believe, well be applied to NATO.
The Alliance has not lost its logic or its usefulness. But the time has
surely come to correct an overextension into the Aegean and Black
seas which, of questionable soundness in the first place, has now
become more of a burden than a source of strength.

IX

Our Western European Friends

THIS BRINGS ME TO THE QUESTION OF OUR GENERAL RELATIONS WITH the members of the hard core of the European Community, which must be taken to include France.

That this relationship has its complications, from our standpoint, is obvious. These lie, in the first instance, in the somewhat neurotic reactions of public opinion in most of those countries, and particularly among the intellectuals, towards the Soviet Union and towards ourselves. This applies above all to Britain, France and the Benelux countries. The Germans, if their radical youth be excepted, are more realistic on both counts.

With respect to the Soviet Union there has been established in the minds of many of the Europeans a certain fixed pattern of thought and assumption. It is a pattern which has eaten its way into their entire outlook on world affairs and on their own position; and they are not to be brought away from it. It consists in the unshakable belief: (1) that the Soviet leaders are, and have been ever since 1945, keenly desirous of launching an attack on Western Europe; (2) that without the commitment of America's nuclear power neither the Western Europeans, nor they and the Americans together, would have the faintest chance of resisting successfully an onslaught of this nature — such is the overwhelming strength of the Soviet Union; and (3) that the Russians have been deterred from launching such an attack only by the threat of American nuclear retaliation. A variant of this view is that the Soviet leadership has it in mind not necessarily to invade Western Europe but only to amass against it such an unanswerable array of superior force that the Western Europeans would see no alternative but to surrender themselves politically, placing themselves in effect at the disposal of the Soviet leaders and inquiring their pleasure.

I shall try to deal more adequately with this persuasion when I come to talk about the Soviet Union. Suffice it to say, here, that no part of this is sound. The assumptions with relation to Soviet intentions are faulty in a number of respects. The assumptions with relation to Soviet strength are as exaggerated as are those that relate to Western European weakness. The belief that stronger powers dominate weaker ones and dictate terms to them simply by the possession of superior military force, or by demands placed under threat of the use of such force, has extremely slender support in historical experience.

To say this is not to suggest that Soviet military strength and intentions present no problem at all — or that they call for no reaction at all from the Western side. It is simply to say that this particular vision: of the Soviet Union confronting Western Europe with overwhelming and wholly unchallengeable force, which the West could never hope successfully to oppose with conventional weaponry, and being deterred only by the American nuclear capability from employing this force either for an attack on Western Europe or for its political intimidation — this is one of those dreadful stereotypes, built of over-simplification and exaggerated apprehension, which so easily come to command the outlooks of large bodies of people. It bears only a faint reality to the problem presented by the real phenomenon of Soviet power.

Yet there it is. The Western Europeans, as I say, are not to be brought away from it. Nor are we, by and large, the people to make the attempt. Too many senior American figures, especially on the military side, have accepted the same conviction and pursue it with the same anxious single-mindedness as their European counterparts.

Well, the fear is real, even if the phantom to which it attaches itself is not; and we have no choice but to indulge it. In this respect, we have to treat our European friends as a species of psychiatric patient with hallucinations. We will get nowhere by trying to persuade him that the hallucinations are not real. We will have to talk and act on his terms, not our own, if we are to get anywhere with him.

This means, of course, that the American military presence in Western Europe cannot be diminished. On the contrary, it should, in its conventional aspects, be increased, unless some real progress can be made in the Mutual and Balanced Force Reduction talks. What is needed here is not so much to give the Western Europeans real military protection (though the United States could and should contribute importantly to that, too) but rather to give them the sense of security they obviously require. The sooner they can be persuaded that our combined conventional power is sufficient to do the trick, or at least to "deter," and that the nuclear potential is not necessary for this purpose, the better; for this will ease the problem — probably the most important problem of international life in this epoch — of bringing nuclear weaponry under control.

As for their attitude towards us: it also has its neurotic quality. This is the reflection, of course, of the disparity between our apparent strength in the world, industrially and militarily, and their own sense of weakness. As little as a hundred years ago, three of these countries of Western Europe viewed themselves as great powers. It is hard, now, for them to accustom themselves to their present position, particularly because they have, for the most part, never fully understood the extent to which their present relative weakness is the product of their own fratricidal slaughter in the two world wars. Seldom do they push through to the recognition that what is really wrong with them is not any sudden loss of quality or injustice of fate but the absence of the many millions of men, then the cream of their youth, who fell in the two world wars. This failure of understanding gives rise to a bewilderment which provides fertile ground for aberration in the assessment of their relationship to both of the present "great powers": the Soviet Union and the United States.

Their reactions towards us Americans, in any case, are ones that we can hope to meet only in limited degree. For as far as they are concerned, we are damned if we do and damned if we don't. If we pay attention to them, we are accused of trying to dominate them. If we leave them alone, we are reproached for neglect. We serve, moreover, as the scapegoat for those weaknesses which they dislike in themselves but are unable to control. Because we were the first to absorb many of the insidious temptations of the modern industrial society — mass culture, automobiles, sensationalism and vulgarization of every sort — they find it convenient to blame us for the fact that they are now affected by the same things. Voluntarily, and of their own decision, they import the worst of American culture, then reproach us for being the origin of it. Because of our relative economic and financial weight, it is always tempting and easy to look for the source of their own economic and financial difficulties in America's behavior. In many matters of international organization and policy, they anxiously solicit our opinion and then charge us, when we give it, of trying to dictate to them. We serve, finally, in our brashness, our slouchy word-slurring casualness, and our frequent vulgarity, as the reassurance (which they desperately need) of the superiority of their own cultural tradition.

There is little we can do about all this, other than to try not to play up to it more than we have to. And it need not worry us beyond a point. For all this edginess and for all their criticism of us, these people are, for the most part, our best friends, almost our only friends — not in the sense that they like us, individually or collectively, but in the sense that they know us well, after so many mutual involvements; that they are aware, as are few others in this world, of their stake in the existence and the prospering (spiritually as well as economically) of our society; that they are conscious, in other words, of the community of fate that binds us all together and makes inconceivable, or difficult of conception, a promising future of the one without the other. There are not many other peoples in the world of whom all that can be said. We have no choice but to value the relationship and to do what we can, even to the point of military defense, to see them through — always, of course, to the extent they will let us do it and will reciprocate the sense of obligation.

All this is just to say that I view our stake in their security as one of the very few really vital interests this country possesses, and would rather see us concentrate our efforts on meeting and protecting it than waste them on a thousand peripheral efforts in other parts of the world.

To say this is not to ignore, however, the great question marks that lie over the future of the countries of Western Europe — question marks which, should they find their answers in the wrong way, could alter the whole basis for our relationship. The preponderant tendency of these societies in recent years has been in the direction of the welfare state — of a humane (for the moment) but highly bureaucratic and egalitarian socialism. This tendency seems now to be approaching certain limits beyond which it cannot go. Other answers will presumably have to be found. The limits that have been reached are in part those of expense; for it is simply not possible to go on indefinitely, giving more and more in the way of social security to people who work less and less. But beyond this, the tendency seems to be approaching certain political limits as well; for it steadily enhances the power of the bureaucracy and of the labor unions at the expense of the parliament — of the professional representative at the expense of the political one. What emerges is, as George Ball has pointed out in his book *Diplomacy in a Crowded World*, something resembling a corporate organization of society, in which the powers of the elected representatives of the people are severely limited by those of the bureaucracy and — what is even worse, for here power is wholly divorced from responsibility — the unions. Worst of all is the fact that this organization of society, in which the people are given a somewhat debilitating social security in return for the abandonment of much of their real influence on political decision, does not seem to produce very much in the way of outstanding personal leadership. The very egalitarianism militates against it. No substitute seems to have been found for the statesman of earlier ages whose courage, self-confidence and largeness of spirit were conditioned by personal wealth and assured family position. Whether, in these circumstances (and it is a question which applies to ourselves as well), the leadership will be found to move the respective peoples out of the smug materialism and cultural inanity (in part even decadence) of the welfare state, and to restore tone, morale, and a sense of purpose to lethargic, overprotected and overcomfortable societies, seems doubtful. Yet unless it is found, one sees no satisfactory channel of exit by democratic means from the blind alley into which the European welfare state seems now to be entering.

Sooner or later people will begin to react in various ways to this strange and, in the long run, intolerable situation. One of the first of these reactions may be seen (at least so we may suspect) in the bizarre tendency to national, ethnic, or linguistic particularism that has now overcome considerable portions of the Western European populations. The desire of the Scotch and Welsh (not to mention Northern Ireland) to set themselves off from the main body of the British community; the petty squabbles of the two Belgian linguistic communities; the demands of such groups as the Basques, the Bretons, and the hill folk of the Juras for a new political identity distinguished from that of the larger national entities to which they now belong; the demands of a minority of the Norwegian population that the entire language of the country be changed to eliminate the effects of the earlier Danish influence: these and other such phenomena surely reflect the search for a more meaningful collective identity than any the modern welfare state has been able to provide. They must be presumed to be the expression of a pathetic desire to escape from the very blandness of the materialistic and secular welfare society of the modern age, and to tap, from earlier and more local roots, something of the faith and vitality of their ancestors. They are a re-action, in other words, against the meaningless "larger" of the present, and a retreat into the idealized "smaller" of the past, and in that sense, a mute, irrational, not even fully conscious revolt against the welfare society. It will not, we must expect, be the last of such struggles at emancipation. What forms the further ones will take, we cannot know.

The way in which Western European society is going is one, in other words, to which we cannot see the ending and in the face of which, for the moment, we stand largely helpless, except insofar as we might be able to help by example — a possibility we have thus far singularly failed to develop. That such uncertainty surrounds their future does not constitute a reason for any weakening of our defense commitment to them at the present juncture. It does suggest a very careful and thoughtful attention to their further development, not only because it is a case, in part, of "there but for the grace of God go we," but also because the tendencies just noted could, if carried too far, eventually undermine the rationale of Western Europe's military defense — for them no less than for us.

I have spoken thus far about Western Europe in general terms. Here, too, of course, generalization is useful only to a point. It might help to complete the picture, therefore, if one were to glance briefly at some of the individual components of this regional community.

1. FRANCE

Many anxieties are being expressed, at this moment of writing, about the political future of France. Here, once more, the Communist Party seems closer than it has been for many years to a partici-pation in government, in coalition with the Socialists. Here again, as in Italy, the danger suggests itself that even a portion of the governmental power might place the Communist leaders in a position where they could contrive to disembarrass themselves of their Socialist partners, to seize the commanding position of political power, and to attain the dictatorial power to which, for so long, they aspired. The fact that they now renounce any such intention, and profess to have discovered the virtues of a pluralistic political society, is not generally seen as much of a reassurance; for the change of opinion is too recent, and too obviously tactically inspired, to be wholly convincing; and even if it were sincere, the discipline of political competition and the fear of repudiation could easily move them to return to a political philosophy in the spirit of which the Party was reared and with which it has been impregnated for some fifty years. These apprehensions are fortified by the fact that the French Communist Party has a much larger component of sincere Stalinists in its rank and file than does its Italian counterpart.

Again, the danger lies not so much in the relations of a successful French Communist Party with Moscow as in its relations with NATO and the remainder of Western Europe. For the leadership of the Party, despite the strong Stalinist slant of a portion of its rank and file, has already gone some distance in emancipating itself from Russian tutelage, and would certainly go much farther if its position was stiffened by governmental responsibility. Relations with the remainder of the NATO community would of course be less affected than would otherwise have been the case by virtue of the fact that France has for long not been participating in the military activities of the pact. Nevertheless, she is a central member of the European Community; and the transformation of her society into even an independent and moderate form of Communist state could not help but affect profoundly her relationship to the remainder of the European Community.

A good case can be made, therefore, for the anxieties to which I have just referred. Nevertheless, it is my own feeling that they are probably exaggerated. French society has, to some extent, been polarized ever since the revolution of 1789 into its radical-Jacobin and royalist-conservative factions, with severe and sometimes dramatic vacillations between the predominance of one or the other. The immediate future would appear to be another time of high tension. But there are also great unifying and restraining forces in French society which militate against extremism in either direction. The normal functioning of the French state is assured by the finest, best-educated, most powerful and most competent of all modern bureaucracies — so much so that it is difficult to conceive of anyone's attempting to rule France without its help. And the fierce competitiveness and individualism of French society make it difficult for any one segment of French society to establish a total dominion over any other.

The French resemble in many respects the Chinese: highly intelligent, exquisitely civilized, outstandingly competent — even to the point of talent — but hard, and not incapable of ruthlessness when too severely challenged. They too have a strong sense of the superiority of their own culture, a feeling of being the "middle kingdom" in European terms, and a not inconsiderable streak of xenophobia (though when they are your friends, you may search the world and not find better). And they are passionate individualists, fiercely attached to what they consider to be their rights.

All in all, then, they are not a people easily pushed around; and there is reason to have confidence in their ability to continue to carry on in their own tradition, Communists or no Communists. There is even reason to suppose that should the Communists come, in one way or another, to power, France would change them more than they would change France.

Despite all the depreciation of us and all the complaints about our alleged desire to dominate them, the French, in their hearts, have accepted us; and they are in that sense our friends. This does not mean that we should pander to them or put up with unreasonableness at their hands. They themselves do not act that way with one another; and they do not expect it of others. It does mean that we should carry forward our differences with them in the way they under-

[131]

stand: emphatically, firmly, but politely and with underlying respect. If that is done, we should continue to find them, generally speaking, on our side in the more decisive questions of international affairs.

2. THE GERMANS

No great people of the modern age, unless it be the Russian, has undergone over the past century such a shattering series of traumatic experiences as the German. First, after 1871, the heady wine of national unity after centuries of fragmentation; then the tragic effort of World War I, followed by the humiliations of an unjust and vindictive peace, inflicted on a new democratic government which had had no part in the responsibility for the war; then the tremendous ups and downs of the Weimar period — the alternation between hope and despair, feverish and wildly creative cultural life against the background of inflation, extremist impatience, and finally the most dreadful of all economic recessions; then the excitements and enticements ot Nazism, culminating in the failure of a second major war effort in a generation; finally, military collapse, occupation, partition of the country and the capital — amid the wreckage of every national idea, every great undertaking, every institution, every political experiment experienced in the course of three generations. Small wonder that in the wake of these disasters the people of Western Germany have lived, since 1945, as in a dream, a comfortable enough dream physically (too comfortable, almost), but unreal, unsubstantial, and with a terrifying sense of the shakiness of the ground beneath.

In the life of the German Federal Republic, echoes of all these earlier phases of German life still reverberate and still influence, sometimes even determine, the conduct of people. But none predominates; none is convincing; none marks a plausible way into the future. In the face of this vacuum, most Germans have seen nothing to do but to go on working and living, in the physical sense, playing their part in a new, quite tolerable, but unexciting political system suggested for them by the Americans, yet seeing no higher purpose, no goal to which it is all tending, no focal point for idealism, duty, or commitment. Against this background, the phenomena of materialism, uncertainty, and cynicism, which have emerged so prominently on the German scene, are not surprising. Surprising, only that they have not been worse.

In a great many respects, the Germans have not done badly, either socially, or economically, or even in the military sense. In point of employment, labor peace, and control of inflation, they have been among the leaders of Europe. They have contrived to restore military strength without restoring militarism. Today, with the French out of it, the British almost prostrate, and the southern tier of NATO in the disarray we have just had occasion to observe, they stand, in fact, as most of what there is to the European leg of NATO. They have developed a highly stable political system, and made it work. The old political extremisms of communism and National Socialism are still there, but are insignificant in strength. This is more than the Western allies, as they moved to the restoration of Western Germany in the late 1940s, deserved or could have hoped for.

The situation is not all rosy. The violent radicalism of a considerable portion of German student youth in recent years contrasts strangely with the mild inoffensiveness of governmental power. And the helplessness — the lack of self-confidence — of the constituted authorities in the face of these new symptoms of potential totalitarianism which the violent youthful radicalism represents has been extraordinary. It is not easy to understand how the Berlin Senate, for example, could have sat passively by and witnessed, without serious counteraction, the destruction, by the most brutal and physical means, of all that part of the Free University of that city that had to do with the humanities. But both these phenomena can be explained, actually, by that dreamlike, unreal quality of post-1945 German life — that lack of a firm foundation of belief and hope and objective — that we have just noted. Youth rebels at the acceptance of a spiritual vacuum. Age, when all the old standards are shattered, lacks the sureness of touch to know how to deal with the rebellion.

Today, the Germans, whether or not the other Europeans like it, are the strength of Western Europe, militarily and economically. They occupy the central position in the effort to which the United States has been committed ever since 1947: to shore up the vitality and self-confidence and the capacity for leadership of these old European peoples, who have constituted for centuries back the heart of Europe's tremendous culture. Without the Germans there would be, today, little for us to build on.

Our relations with Western Germany, therefore, are nothing to be taken casually. There is little we can do in any direct way to support the Germans, still less to lead them to a more hopeful and inspiring view of their own future. But they are among the least anti-American of the European peoples. They have a keen interest in our civilization, and are highly sensitive to our example. (If we could only realize, as we shape our national life at home, that we are also, thereby, shaping in part the strength of our international relationships, we could do more for our security in the world than by the fanciest theories of "massive retaliation" or "deterrence" or "assured destruction" or what you will.)

We do not do badly, as it is today, in our relations with the Western Germans. They are in fact, of all our Western European allies, the easiest to relate to. But no more than others can they be taken for granted. They are a people of tremendous physical and social vitality — a vitality bound, at this delicate juncture, when the necessities of physical recovery from the disaster of the great war are wearing thin as a motive for individual activity, to strike out on new paths. These paths could be good; they could be bad. Our example will be an important factor in determining which it shall be.

[134]

3. BRITAIN

In the present condition of Britain we have the most extraordinary, the most puzzling, and the most disturbing of the phenomena of European life today. Never, surely, except under the impact of overwhelming military defeat (which the British have not known) has a great country gone so rapidly from world power to extreme helplessness. One can think as one likes about the deeper causes of this sudden decline in national effectiveness (and this is not the place to air my own thoughts about it). The fact is that it has already basically changed the face of Western Europe, as it presents itself to this country, and may change it even more.

The crisis appears to be profound. For many of us it is not possible to see how the deterioration can be halted until either the power of British trade unionism is broken or the unions are forced to accept a responsibility commensurate with their power. One way or another people will have to be brought to accept the necessity of hard work if they are to compete successfully with others in the economic exchanges of the world; and compete they must, for the British Isles, which in happier times could at least have fed themselves and provided out of their own resources many of the other elements of a physical existence, are now overpopulated to a point where they can live successfully only by a high level of exchanges with the outside world.

Again, the United States stands relatively helpless in the face of this situation. Further infusions of credit from outside will not help unless the sources of the difficulty, which lie in the low productivity and vitality of British economic life, are corrected.

There is, however, one thing we *can* do; and that is to show, as never before, a high degree of confidence in the long-term future of British civilization. We have reason to do so; for there is something unnatural, and not fully credible, about the present crisis in British life. No such drastic change in the life of a great people over a short time can be entirely real. A people so great as the British, with all they have given to the world in earlier centuries — with their tremendous literature, their other vast achievements in the fields of culture and science, and a genius of self-government that has lain at the very source of all modern democracy — do not cease to be great in a single generation. The genes would not even permit it. Latent in British society there must be immense sources of vitality and creativity that remain only to be touched in the right way to spring to life and to alter, once again, the whole face of British civilization. Until they do, it is up to us to retain, and to manifest, a confidence in the British people that they might otherwise be inclined to lose in themselves. This, in addition to remaining a loyal ally and standing by for the event that any real chance to help should present itself, will be our best contributions. The British are, for all the vicissitudes of fortune, along with the Canadians the closest and most reliable friends we have in this world.

4. THE SMALLER PEOPLES

Not to be neglected, when we think of Western Europe, are the smaller countries of that region, not just the NATO members — the Benelux countries and the Scandinavian ones — but also Sweden, Switzerland, and Austria. They are all vulnerable to a large extent, particularly the Dutch and the Danes, to the growing problems of the welfare state. None of them views us (and for this we may be thankful) with any particular sentimentality. Some are not even formally our allies. Yet they all constitute a vital part of the Europe on the prosperity and endurance of which our security depends.

To those of them that are officially neutral, we have, of course, no formal commitment. Actually, their security is no less important to us than that of the countries to whose defense we are committed. They want no guarantee from us; and none should be suggested. But they appreciate, as do very few countries of the Third World, the importance, and generally speaking the positive nature, of our contribution to world affairs. They know that, as great powers go, they can be lucky that we are no worse than we are. And the cultural ties by which they are bound to us, and we to them, are fruitful ones, and of high importance.

There is nothing we can do to strengthen our relations with them other than to refrain from neglecting them or underrating them. Several American presidents have evidently concluded that because they were small in size and population, their capitals represented places to which the less qualified and less impressive of political appointees could well be sent as ambassadors. There could be no greater error. Nowhere is an American representative more conspicuous — nowhere do ignorance, provincialism and lack of experience stand out more unfortunately — than in the capitals of these small but highly cultured countries, whose contribution, past and present, to the greatness of Europe can hardly be overrated. They are not only a part of our world, but one of its greatest and most significant parts, and should be viewed accordingly.

5. THE EURO-AMERICAN ECONOMIC PROBLEMS

The larger part of the official exchanges between the U.S. government and the countries of Western Europe relate to economic and financial matters. This is, in fact, most of what the Europeans talk about among themselves. This ssems to be characteristic of the leaders of the welfare states. Unsure of themselves in the great political questions, they feel on firmer ground when they can dig into such questions as the price of wine and carrots, or the intricate interrelationships of exchange rates. Which observation should not be taken as a suggestion that these things are not important, but only as a reminder that behind the cloud of these abstruse and complex squabbles, the larger issues, which in the end are apt to be decisive, get neglected.

Just as the Western Europeans, in any case, turn the face of their economic complaints and necessities to one another, so they turn it to us, sometimes with good reason, sometimes because we, with our great economic weight, make a very good scapegoat to blame things on. And we customarily do our best to respond — although usually with some difficulty, because most of the questions that arise in this field have strong domestic-political connotations in Washington, and they occasion, once raised, longer and more difficult negotiations within the Washington political establishment than with our foreign partners.

It is idle for anyone attempting to think about the broader issues of American foreign policy to undertake to comment in detail on the many individual questions that arise in this field. They are highly complex. They change rapidly. As a rule, they cannot be understood without specialized knowledge. And they are habitually, and probably inevitably, handled at the Washington end not from the standpoint of America's world-political interests but from the standpoint of their impacts on various American lobbies, interest groups, and individual political ambitions.

Many of the demands with which our Western European friends importune us are clearly unjust. Here, too, in many instances, we are damned if we do and damned if we don't: damned for not controlling inflation, damned (by implication, at least) for controlling it too much; damned for fixing an exchange rate, damned for letting one float. We cannot satisfy all these demands; nor should their frequent unreasonableness upset us.

But in general, we should be concerned to show generosity and understanding in our dealings with the Europeans in this field. The place where we could help most significantly, psychologically as well as economically, would be in the overcoming of the worst examples of protectionism. But this, clearly, is a domestic-political matter. All that can be asked of the Executive branch is that it continue to sweat such questions out as it has done in the past, not forgetting, meanwhile, the importance of educating the public, as only the White House can do, to the broader negative implications of protectionist policies.

X

Eastern Europe

BEFORE WE COME TO THE SUBJECT OF SOVIET RUSSIA — THE CENTRAL problem of American foreign policy — it will be well to have a glance at the band of peoples and political authorities that lies between the democratic countries of Western Europe and the boundaries of the Soviet Union.

1. YUGOSLAVIA

There are two of these countries that have to be set firmly aside from the others. They simply cannot be treated in the same breath. And the first of these is Yugoslavia.

It seems incredible, nearly thirty years after the break between Tito and Stalin and the attendant establishment of Yugoslavia's independence (initially from Moscow alone and later from the entire Warsaw Pact bloc), that one should find oneself still obliged to emphasize that that country is not under Soviet domination, that it has no significant political or military ties to Moscow, that it does not belong to the Warsaw Pact, that it leads a wholly independent existence, and that while its leaders are the product of a Marxist upbringing and still call themselves, by force of habit and for want of a better word, "Communists," the way of life of the Yugoslav peoples bears very little similarity to that of their Soviet counterparts — is, in fact, closer to that of certain of the Western peoples than to that of the Soviet Union. I would not feel it necessary to call attention to these rather elementary and generally well-known facts had I not, when serving as ambassador to Yugoslavia some years ago, been obliged to argue long and futilely with certain of our legislators in the effort to convince them that things were really this way; and had not President Ford, in his campaign utterances, thrown some doubt on his own understanding of these facts by grouping Yugoslavia uncritically with Poland and Rumania.

One of the sources of the confusion of American opinion on this subject, aside from the continued occasional employment by the Yugoslavs of the term "Communist," is perhaps the common aberration of assuming that whoever is not with us must be against us. For while it is true that Tito is not — or, better, is only partly — Moscow's friend, so it is also true that he is only partly ours. As an ideologist, he is closer to Moscow. As a nationalist, concerned to protect his own political independence and that of his peoples, he is perhaps closer to us. His words have a tendency to tilt to the East, his actions to the West. In bilateral relations he treats us, as a rule, fairly and in a manner to which no one could object. In the forum of world politics he associates himself, enthusiastically and uncritically, with our worst enemies in the Third World.

In these circumstances, our relations with Yugoslavia are subject to limitations. We cannot wholly forget the generally anti-American posture of the group of "non-aligned" nations, of which Tito has been from the start the outstanding leader. And we also have to recognize certain domestic-political inhibitions of our own in dealing with the Yugoslav regime; for it is unfortunately a fact that the anti-Tito Yugoslavs, or persons of Yugoslav origin, residing in this country have been very successful in commending themselves to American sympathies on the strength of a professed "anti-communism," and have succeeded time and again in bending American policy in an anti-Titoist direction that has interfered unnecessarily with our relations with Yugoslavia and has corresponded to no American (as distinct from Croatian or Serbian or Slovene) interest.

Tito is now no longer young; the vigor of his leadership is no longer entirely what it once was; and it is not unnatural that people should begin to think about the day when he will no longer be able to give to that country the firm and skillful leadership he has given to it for so many years. This has led to some strange speculations and visions, including not only that of a breakup of the country into its several ethnic parts but also that of a possible Soviet invasion, conquest, and subsequent incorporation into the body of the Warsaw Pact. These latter apprehensions have found a particularly prominent place in the reports of the European correspondent and columnist of the *New York Times*, Mr. Cyrus Sulzberger. And they appear, from his campaign statements, even to have impressed Mr. Carter, prior to his election to office.

As to the first of these fears, that relating to a possible breakup of the country: the only judgment that can be given is: possible but not probable. There is no love lost among the several ethnic components of the Yugoslav population. Indeed, the country, as established at the end of the First World War, was a highly artificial creation. There could, conceivably, have been better solutions at that time. But the various Yugoslav peoples have now contrived to live alongside each other, within the same sovereign framework, for over half a century; and in some respects the rudiments of a national identity have been established. None of these peoples, in any case, could today look forward to anything resembling a satisfactory future as an isolated, independent entity. There is in fact not one of them which, if it tried to go it alone, would not at once be faced with dangerous irredentist demands on the part of individual neighbors — demands which it, in its isolated state, would be quite unable to withstand.

It is difficult to believe that the logic of this situation would not impress itself upon the leaders of the various ethnic components of the Yugoslav population, even in the absence of Tito's leadership. That his absence would lead, initially, to considerable instability in Yugoslav governmental affairs is not at all improbable, because it has been his hand that for thirty years has dominated political life and held the country together. And it would be idle to suggest that this situation would not have its dangers. But that the leaders of the centrifugal forces operating in Yugoslav society today would be so shortsighted as to embark on the suicidal folly of a civil war and invite the miseries of foreign intervention from virtually every side of Yugoslavia's long borders, seems something less than probable.

As for the possibility of Soviet intervention: some of the assumptions that seem to underlie the professed fears on this score are clearly on the wild side. That the Soviet leaders should be panting to invade Western Europe is far-reaching enough as an estimate of their intentions. That they should be seen as simultaneously anxious to mount a similar invasion of Yugoslavia reaches farther into the realm of pure fancy. At no time in the near thirty years since the Stalin-Tito break has this been a serious danger. If danger exists at all in this direction, it lies in the possibility that the end of the Tito regime might, after all, unleash serious centrifugal tendencies in Yugoslav political life; that one or another of the Eastern European countries (Bulgaria being the most likely candidate) might see in this a favorable opportunity for an effort to recover, or incorporate, certain of the portions of the present Yugoslav territory that it covets; and that the Russians might then feel compelled to support the protégé in question, and thus be dragged into the fracas. This, again, is a possible but not probable scenario; and no good will be done by making it the subject of extravagant and panic-inducing speculation.

The Yugoslavs are among the world's finest soldiers. They have the third strongest army in the non-Soviet-dominated part of Europe. This army is well prepared to resist an invader on the plains, and even better prepared to retire to the mountains and to put up, there, a resistance far stronger than was offered to the Germans by the Yugoslav partisans during the last world war (and they, it must be remembered, held up a respectable number of German divisions). This armed strength was not created as a protection for the West; but the geographic position of Yugoslavia makes it so. The nature, disposition, and location of Tito's Yugoslavia has been, whether or not he wished it to be that way, of inestimable advantage to the NATO community in keeping Soviet and Warsaw Pact forces at a distance from the Adriatic Sea and from the territory of NATO members.

The West, therefore, including the United States, has an important stake in the continued existence and prospering of the Yugoslav state as we now know it. We will be well advised not to weaken that state by the abuse of our relations with it (as so many of the Yugoslav-Americans would have us do), or by a sort of gloating speculation on the dangers it might undergo with the departure of Tito. The United States, in particular, should bear in mind that it has, in the person of the Yugoslav population, one of the least anti-American, indeed one of the most touchingly friendly and kindly in its relationship to our country, of all the world's peoples. This is an asset we should not lightly abuse.

2. FINLAND

Such is the distorting effect of the extreme bipolarity marking so much of Western opinion that people seem to have difficulty understanding the position of any European country which finds itself obliged to stand somewhere between the Communist and the non-Communist worlds. This, unfortunately, affects Finland as it does Yugoslavia.

No greater injustice has been done to any European people than has been done to the Finns by the bandying about, in Western Euro-

pean and American usage, of the concept of the possible "Finlandiza-
tion" of Western Europe, with the implication that this means some
sort of helpless and humiliating situation vis-à-vis the Soviet Union — not formal absorption into the Soviet bloc but a spineless acceptance of Soviet domination and willingness to accept Soviet dicta-
tion in all essential aspects of political life. One may have one's
opinions as to the likelihood, or necessity, of Western Europe's ever
accepting such a position; but certainly it is incorrect, and unjust in
highest degree, to impute it to the Finns. The policy they have followed towards the Soviet Union since the recent war has been, for
obvious reasons, a prudent and restrained one. They have showed
themselves concerned not to become a problem for the Soviet Union
and not to lend themselves in any way to the efforts of others to
make trouble for Moscow. Certain of the Western European governments which declared war on Finland and then pressed the Finns to
surrender to the Russians in 1944 should be the last to reproach
them for this prudence.

But the fact is that beyond these well-warranted policies of restraint, the Finns have conducted themselves vis-à-vis the Soviet
Union with a remarkable dignity, with cool nerves and composure,
and with a quiet but firm and successful insistence on the right to
lead their own lives, internally, after their own fashion and in accord
with their own principles. In no way have they deserved to be held
up as the example of a humiliating subservience to a larger power.

Culturally and spiritually, in their habits and inclinations, the
Finns are a part of the Western world, which does not imply a mili-
tant hostility to any other. They should be thought of in much the
same way as the other European neutrals. We have no commitment
to their defense; and no good purpose would be served by our trying
to interest ourselves in it. It is the essence of their situation that they
themselves must contrive to assure, with such means as they have,
their own security. We can help them only by giving them our respect for their remarkable accomplishments as a people, and our understanding for their unique and delicate geographic situation. And

we may usefully bear in mind that this, a country whose friendship we should value, is one of the countries whose interests we jeopardize when we give too bipolar an interpretation to our conflicts with the Soviet Union and act as if the only people whose interests were affected by those conflicts were ourselves and our NATO partners.

3. THE COMMUNIST EASTERN EUROPE

Between the non-Communist countries of Europe, including (for purposes of this discussion) the Yugoslavs, and the borders of the Soviet Union, we have, as specific problems for American foreign policy, the six Communist-controlled Eastern European countries of the Warsaw Pact group. They present a somewhat different problem than does the Soviet Union itself, and warrant a special examination.

The first thing to be noted about these countries is the extent of the differences they exhibit, as political personalities. The day is long past when they could be viewed, and treated, as a uniform phenomenon. No two of them are entirely alike either in their relations with the Soviet Union or in the picture they present to us. Their political situations, too, are not the same in any two instances. All, one must suppose, except possibly Eastern Germany, are held in the Soviet orbit strongly against the will of their peoples. In certain instances they are held against the secret desires of their Communist rulers as well. In other cases, the rulers have to welcome the continuance of Soviet domination because without the support it implies they would not have the faintest chance of continuing in power, or even avoiding personal catastrophe. Certain of these countries have Soviet forces stationed on their territory. Others do not. Some participate prominently in the activities of the Warsaw Pact, others less so, the Rumanians very little. The first requirement of American policy with relation to them is, therefore, that it not blind itself to these differences but that it be intelligently differentiated.

[146]

The second thing to be borne in mind when considering the problem these countries present for American foreign policy is the ambivalence that they present in every significant aspect of their personality. The United States cannot act as though all that was involved in this relationship were the governments. But similarly it cannot act as though all that was important were the attitudes of the peoples. The governments are all linked to, and in some ways dependent upon, the Soviet connection. The peoples are, almost to a man, anti-Russian if not anti-Communist. Both have to be taken into account. There is thus an ambiguity as between governments and peoples. Even the most anti-Communist of foreign statesmen cannot go too far in opposing the governments without bringing injury or hardship to the peoples as well. But he cannot go too far in bringing comfort to the peoples without benefiting the governments as well.

Nor is this ambiguity confined to the dichotomy of government versus people. The governing Communist elites themselves are torn in their feelings, anxious in some respects to guard the Russian tie, in other respects to weaken it. An over-simplified, single-minded Western approach, if on the hard side, can discourage their efforts to achieve a more flexible and independent position; if on the soft side, it can make it easier for them to have their cake and eat it too in the sense of continuing to pursue oppressive policies towards their own people, and subservient ones towards Moscow, and still enjoying to some extant the favor and support of the non-Communist West.

Thus the first requirement of a sound American policy towards these countries is that it should be sensitively differentiated, as among the various states in question, and carefully balanced, as between conflicting considerations. This means that nowhere are the sort of blanket restrictions and prescriptions which flow from congressional determinations less in place than with relation to this region. If policy is to be effective here, the Executive branch must be free to make fine and sensitive day-by-day decisions, geared to the shifts and changes of the moment. Any rigid policy, incapable of reaction to unpredictable events, will be self-defeating.

[147]

All of the above relates to the situation we have before us today. One must also consider the problems that might be posed for us by extensive changes in the status quo now prevailing in that region. These could be of three kinds: either the overthrow of one of the Communist regimes, or its failure to such an extent as to necessitate renewed Russian intervention and occupation of the country, or the success of one of the existing Communist regimes in establishing, as did Tito and as almost did at one time both Imre Nagy and Alexander Dubček, a virtual independence of Soviet control, implying, or threatening, a departure from the ranks of the Warsaw Pact.

Except in the case of Poland, where the future of the relations between the regime and the working population is uncertain, there is little likelihood of any realization of the first two of these possibilities in the foreseeable future. The third one, namely, some form of self-emancipation from Moscow by one of the Communist regimes, is perhaps more of a possibility, particularly in the light of the extensive changes in the Soviet leadership which must be expected to take place in the next two or three years. And it is worth noting that the NATO powers are very poorly equipped to react to it. Both the Hungarian events of 1956 and the Czechoslovak crisis of 1968 caught them quite off guard and without effective response. One of the drawbacks of the present rigid division of Europe, and the rejection by the Western powers of any thought of disengagement, is that it leaves those powers devoid both of ideas and of flexibility of action in the face of any serious disruption of the solidarity of the Eastern Bloc. As things now stand, one must suppose that if any of the Eastern European countries was suddenly to emancipate itself from the Soviet tutelage and to require that a new place be found for it in the European scheme of things, the Western NATO powers would be no less appalled by such a development than the leaders of the Soviet Union. They, too, have committed themselves to the present line of division.

The East European countries' armed forces enter prominently, of course, into the calculations of the East-West military balance, which is today such a lively object of concern and debate in NATO circles. But many of the values assigned to those forces in these calculations are either unreal or highly uncertain. Much might depend on the way in which hostilities broke out. In the event of a sudden and unprovoked Soviet attack on the West, none of these countries, except possibly Eastern Germany and Bulgaria (where the aims would be purely local) would have their hearts in the operation. Least of all can it be said that they are "poised" (this is the word that is sometimes used) for an attack on the West, awaiting only the word from Moscow. All this is too unreal to warrant serious discussion. Any aggression by the Soviet Union against the NATO countries would have to use lines of communication across the territory of at least two of the Eastern European satellites. The use of these facilities would have to be prepared some time in advance, which would virtually preclude the advantages of surprise. The Soviet Union cannot simply make use of the territory and peoples of these countries as though their governments and their people consisted solely of automatons, thirsting to do their bidding and so profoundly committed to Soviet leadership that they would blindly and enthusiastically throw themselves into the execution of any Soviet order — as though, in short, they had no national feelings, interests, or reactions of their own.

One of the first requirements of a sensible and effective policy towards the problem of Russian-led communism would be a realistic and sophisticated assessment of the strengths and the weaknesses of the satellite countries as adjuncts to Soviet policy and to Soviet military potential.

XI

═══════════

The Soviet Union—The Alarm

Now, FINALLY WITH THESE VARIOUS OTHER ELEMENTS OF THE WORLD scene in mind, it is time to turn to the central problem of American foreign policy — a problem which exceeds all the others in importance and complexity, and on the approach to which many other facets of American policy depend.

1. "Détente" and Its Misinterpretation

Some years ago, towards the end of the 1960s, for a variety of reasons, among which Russia's relations with China and the consolidation of the authority of the Brezhnev regime played a prominent part, prospects improved for an effort by the U.S. government to reach a better understanding with the Soviet government on a limited but important group of questions. These included outstandingly those of the control of strategic nuclear weaponry — also, those of the possible extension and improvement of exchanges and facilities for collaboration in various commercial and cultural fields.

The Johnson administration made a rather tentative and faint-hearted start at exploring the possibilities of progress along these lines, but the adverse repercussions of the Czechoslovak events of 1968, together with our own involvement in Vietnam, plus the lateness of the hour, politically, for Mr. Johnson himself, restricted severely what that administration was able to accomplish. Nevertheless, the foundations were laid for the SALT talks, and progress was made in two or three other not unimportant areas (particularly airline connections and the expansion of consular representation).

As the trauma of the Czechoslovak events receded and our own Vietnam involvement ground to an end, the new Nixon administration found itself in a relatively favorable situation to pursue these efforts. Mr. Kissinger's exceptional imagination and power of initiative provided a peculiarly effective motive power for the undertaking. Mr. Nixon's earlier record of flaming anti-communism served to disarm the political right wing, always apprehensive and alert, lest peace should break out. What followed is a matter of common knowledge: the SALT talks; the Kissinger and Nixon visits to Moscow; the various bilateral agreements in commercial and cultural fields.

All this soon became known, for some reason, by a special name: *détente*. The name itself was not new, but its use in just this connection caught on mightily with the press and promptly became attached to the efforts just described, as though *they* were something wholly new. To many people the name soon came to signify a general change in Soviet-American relations — a basic turning of the corner, distinguishing this phase of the relationship from all that had gone on before. This impression was then deepened by the histrionics of the various summit meetings. Neither of the two governments concerned (though in each case for different reasons) was averse to letting the impression stand that what was involved here was a major and historical change, promising a new era in the relations between the two countries and between Russia and the West, generally. The press, of course, loved all this, systematically over-dramatized it, and magnified it, in its usual fashion, to several times life size.

The pursuit and conclusion by Messrs. Nixon and Kissinger of useful agreements between the two governments in several specific areas was not in itself unfortunate; what *was* unfortunate was the misimpression conveyed to the public of the significance of what was done. These efforts did not, actually, fall outside the long-established pattern of American policy. There had always been ups and downs in this relationship, defining at each juncture the limits of the possible in the way of their improvement; and the United States government had naturally been concerned, at all times except possibly at the height of the Cold War in the early 1950s, to take advantage of the more favorable opportunities.

It may well be that the early 1970s were a uniquely favorable time for progress in certain directions. But the change was one of degree, not of substance. And the fields in question remained limited. The Soviet authorities never gave reason to suppose that they were willing to depart significantly from their established policies and practices in the suppression of political opposition within the Soviet Union, or in the encouragement of pseudo-Marxist "national liberation movements" in the Third World, or in the continued development of their armed forces in areas not covered by specific arms-control agreements. That government was prepared to conclude agreements with us in specific and limited areas. It reserved its freedom of action in areas not covered by the respective agreements, and gave us no serious reason to assume that its conduct in those other areas would be significantly affected by what people sometimes called "the atmosphere of détente." For the contrary impression we had our own press, and the confusing euphoria of summitry, to thank.

Both governments, perhaps, could be held at fault for not moving to correct the growing impression that some all-pervasive change had occurred by virtue of which the Soviet government would now cease to behave like the Soviet government. But the United States government had no reason to deceive itself on this score. Nor did media of communications commanding such great resources as those of the United States have any excuse for peddling an impression which, as the most rudimentary study of the historical facts would have shown, had no foundation in fact.

Nevertheless, by the time of Watergate, the damage had been done. Large parts of American opinion had been led to expect something that was not to be. And the reaction was not long coming. The achievements of "détente," once the vertigo induced by the summit meetings had passed and the press had turned its magnifying glass on other events, now began to appear insignificant (more so, actually, than was deserved); whereas the continued pursuit by the Soviet authorities of practices in other fields that were disagreeable in American eyes caused displeasure in some American circles and disillusionment in others. This, in turn, was happily seized upon by numbers of people who had never wanted improved relations with the Soviet Union in the first place.

These last were a varied but numerous and vociferous band. Their ranks included those who had an interest of one sort or another in military expenditures; those whose long-standing dream had been to see the United States committed to the overthrow of Soviet power; and those for whom a ringing show of anti-Communist belligerence and vigilance was the stock of political trade. It included others who were wholly unselfish and dedicated in motive but who had a highly bipolar view of international problems and whose suspicions of the Soviet leadership, and hopes for the establishment of American military superiority, were such that they were inclined to see great and dangerous chinks in any arms agreement to which the Soviet government was likely to set its signature; they thus preferred to see us go the path of all-out military preparation rather than that of negotiation for arms control. To all this there was added, as the election of 1976 approached, the fact that the apparent breach between the promises of détente and its demonstrable results provided one more convenient weapon for criticism of the outgoing administration. The

[153]

Soviet government made its own contribution to this reaction by its action in Angola, demonstrating its newly acquired ability to project its military presence to distant and peripheral points.

Out of all this there was brewed, then, a powerful current of opinion in the United States, and to some extent in Western Europe, that professed to see Soviet intentions and actions as more menacing than ever before and advocated not only greatly heightened military expenditures and preparations but the adoption by the United States government, in particular, of a hostile, defiant, and challenging attitude towards the Soviet government — an attitude designed to compel the latter, in the end, to change its policies in the direction of ones more suitable to Western interests.

This reaction was compounded by the aftermath of the Helsinki Conference. The curious series of negotiations that ended with the Helsinki summit meeting grew out of the long-standing Soviet pressure for a European security pact. Certain of the Western Europeans thought the Russians should be met halfway, at least to the point of one's consenting to discuss the subject with them, and it was in this way that the talks began. But at no time was anyone in the West really prepared to contemplate a formal security pact that would replace, or cover, the existing NATO and Warsaw Pact arrangements. The talks thus degenerated into a long struggle over various formulations of high principle, which each side would be at liberty to interpret as it wished when it came to the translation of them into day-by-day practice. The final document did not have the character of a series of binding undertakings — rather, that of a long list of principles to which the various parties were willing to subscribe.

The Western powers were immediately attacked for having assented, in this document, to the thesis that the existing boundaries in Europe should not be altered by force. This, it was claimed, was equivalent to a formal abandonment of all of Eastern Europe, including Eastern Germany, to permanent Soviet domination, and was thus a major, unwarranted, and unrequited concession to the Soviet Union. Actually, none of the Western powers had the faintest idea of attempting to alter any of these boundaries by force or any other way, even in the absence of such a declaration; the very thought of any sort of removal of the division of Europe was in fact abhorrent to them. The supposed concession was therefore not a very real one. The Russians, on the other hand, subscribed in at least three places in the Helsinki communiqué to sentiments which, under even the most perfunctory standards of observance, would have ruled out a repetition of the action taken in Czechoslovakia in 1968. They also accepted language relating to human rights which was at least misleading when taken in relation to their established practices. These latter provisions turned out to be somewhat embarrassing to the Soviet government in the months that followed — so much so that it could well be said that if anyone lost the semantic battle which the Helsinki negotiations actually amounted to, it was the Soviet side and not the West.

In the years before Helsinki, I had tried on many occasions to emphasize to our government the folly of attempting to get the Soviet government to sign up to high-sounding general principles, and especially of pursuing such discussion in multilateral forums, under the daily scrutiny of the world press. I had argued that if one really wanted to have useful agreements with that government, these should be highly specific in character, should consist only of a careful and explicit record of what each side was expected to do pursuant to the understanding in question, and should not concern themselves with motives. The negotiations, I further urged, should consist of private, and preferably bilateral, exchanges of views, not of demonstrative airings of opinion before the press.

The Helsinki negotiations violated every one of these principles. This being the case, I personally could see no reason to expect very much to come of them in the way of alteration of the established practices of the Soviet government, particularly in matters where its own political security was at stake. Nevertheless, the results of Helsinki, particularly the perceived gap between implicit promise and actual performance, were seized upon by those who opposed all at-

tempts at negotiation with Moscow, as evidence of the bad faith of
the Soviet side and the impossibility of arriving at useful agreements
with it other than under the pressure of superior military strength.
This, too, added to the reaction against what people had thought of
as détente.

2. THE MILITARY CHARGE

The principal argument for the thesis that détente was a failure and
has brought us into a dangerous position is that which is based on
the alleged developing disbalance between the Soviet armed forces
and defense preparations and our own.

There seems to be no single authoritative statement of this thesis.
The arguments for it have come from a number of sources. In undertaking to summarize it, as I shall presently do, I am basing myself on several of what seem to me to be the more authoritative ver-
sions of the argument. These include, for example, a statement given
to the *New York Times* by Secretary of Defense Donald H. Rumsfeld
shortly before his retirement from that position; a similar statement
made by General Alexander M. Haig, Jr., Supreme Commander of
the European NATO forces; the statement put out in January 1977
by a bipartisan body, the Committee on the Present Danger, the signatories of which included a number of persons formerly in high
position in the departments of Defense or State or the CIA; personal
statements made by one or another of these same persons; and finally, press stories, such as those of Mr. Drew Middleton in the *New
York Times*, which apparently drew their statistical material, if not
their inspiration, from governmental sources. Whether there is a
complete consensus among those who hold, generally speaking, to
this point of view I would not know; but perhaps the following sum-
mary would not do too much injustice to the case they are making.

First: the general state of our defense effort. Our expenditures on defense, it is alleged, have seriously declined and fallen behind those of the Soviet Union. While they have recently increased in dollar terms, they have decreased, allowing for inflation, in "real" terms, so that they are now 14 percent below the level of the early 1960s and a third less than at the peak of the Vietnam War. Measured against the gross national product, they are less than at any time in the last twenty-five years, constituting only 5.75 percent of it, whereas the corresponding Soviet figure is 11 to 13 percent. For six years, now, the Soviet government has outspent us in absolute dollar amounts devoted to defense.

In the field of strategic nuclear weaponry, the Soviet government, it is alleged, has added over 2,000 launchers to its arsenal just since 1965, whereas our own arsenal effectively leveled out in the late 1960s, with the result that theirs now surpasses our own both in numbers (2,300 to 2,163) and in throw-weight. If, furthermore, present trends are projected into the future, Soviet weaponry of this nature must be expected eventually to surpass our own in a number of other respects. This means, it is argued, that the Soviet government will acquire a capability to destroy so much of our arsenal in a first strike that our second-strike response will be enfeebled, and such damage as it could be expected to do to the Soviet Union would be within the range calculated by us to be "acceptable" from the standpoint of the Soviet leadership. The end of such a nuclear exchange would, in other words, leave much of the Soviet economic and military potential, including the long-range strategic arsenal, intact, whereas we would have exhausted our own long-range striking capacity and would have no real choice but to "surrender."

Turning to conventional weaponry, the thesis in question is supported by a number of arguments. Only a few of them can be cited here. Some are derived from comparisons between the American and the Soviet armed force establishments, some from comparisons between the similar establishments of NATO and the Warsaw Pact. Soviet ground forces, the thesis goes, are more than double our own. The Soviet Union has 45,000 tanks to our 8,500. They have also outproduced us in armored personnel carriers and artillery. Their production of tactical aircraft and helicopters now exceeds ours. The Warsaw Pact command has 67 divisions under its authority to NATO's 29.

In the naval field the Soviet Union is said to have outstripped us in development of both surface ships and submarines and to have double the number of ships afloat.

One could continue this list for pages.

To this must be added the charge that the Soviet Union has gone in for civil defense preparations on so massive a scale (one speaks of such things as 35,000 hardened shelters now under construction) as to suggest that they are anticipating an outbreak of hostilities and are determined to place themselves in a position where, having themselves delivered a first nuclear strike, they could survive a nuclear response from our side — it being argued that whereas we would have suffered so and so many tens of millions of dead in this exchange, they would have suffered a smaller number of tens of millions, a prospect portrayed as so reassuring to them that they would not be averse to initiating the exchange in the first place.

What is one to say to this bombardment of alarming statistics?

Some of them are convincing so far as they go, provided the estimates of Soviet strength on which they rest are sound.

Others are in part sound (assuming, again, that the estimates are correct) but in part misleading. From the mere assertion that the Russians have surpassed us in numbers and throw-weight of strategic missiles the reader would scarcely suppose, for example, that we still had in the neighborhood of 10,000 independently targetable offensive warheads directed against the Soviet Union, compared with something like a third this number for the Russians, not to mention some 7,000 so-called tactical nuclear weapons kept by the United States in Western Europe, which exceed those arrayed against them by a similar factor. (The weakest of these "tactical" weapons is said, incidentally, to be three times the strength of the bomb used against Hiroshima.)

Some of the figures, finally, are of such intrinsic unsoundness, and so highly misleading, that one is surprised to find them emanating from responsible circles. This is true, for example, of the comparisons between the strength of the two navies on the basis of the number of "vessels" they have afloat (the term "vessels" being capable of meaning anything from an admiral's barge to an aircraft carrier). It is also true of the dollar figures sometimes cited as indices of the supposed Soviet military expenditures, the figures being drawn, apparently, from our own estimates of what it would have cost us, with our high labor costs and our inflated present prices, to produce in the United States the items we think they have produced in Russia. Obviously, figures derived from such calculations, taking no account of the thousands of differences in costs, methods, and quality of production that mark the two industrial establishments, are not very revealing.

It would surpass the purpose of this discussion to take these various comparative statistics individually under critical scrutiny, although there would be much to be said by way of criticism about a number of them. But there are reasons why this entire exercise of attempting to convey to the public useful impressions about comparative military strength by the citing of such figures is at best a dubious one, and at worst — seriously misleading. The reasons why this is so are so numerous, and in some instances so elementary, that I hesitate to attempt to list them. A few of them may serve to make the point.

Let us remember, first of all, that there are no general criteria (least of all that of sheer numbers) for measuring the relative merits of weapons or units in a hypothetical future encounter. All depends on the time, the place, the purpose, and the manner, at which, for which, or in which, these weapons or units are employed. A weapon effective on defense may be relatively ineffective on offense. A weapon effective on the plains may be useless in mountainous territory. A weapon in the hands of a highly-trained and motivated unit may have a wholly different value than it has in the hands of a differently trained and motivated one. Mere numerical comparisons do not reflect these variables.

Nor is the fact that someone outproduces you in a given branch of weaponry necessarily a sign that you are becoming militarily inferior. The needs of no two powers are alike, if only because no two powers enjoy the same geographic and political situation. The assessment of the needs of one power in a given form of weaponry is not necessarily relevant to the needs of another. It is perfectly possible for one power to have an appreciable numerical inferiority in a given branch of weaponry without this meaning that it is in any way endangered.

Nor is a given type of weaponry always the most suitable defensive response to that same type of weaponry in the hands of someone else. From the fact that the Soviet government may choose to have some 45,000 tanks in its arsenal, it does not follow that we are endangered if we do not have a similar number in ours. Perhaps, for one thing, the Soviet Union has overproduced, as it has sometimes had a tendency to do. But beyond that, even if all those Soviet tanks were in perfect shape, fully operable, and capable of being employed on a certain front, this is not to say that the best response to them would be a similar or superior number of tanks on our part. On the contrary, one hears that anti-tank weapons are now of such effectiveness, and so easy of use, that large-scale tank warfare may be obsolete.

I must point out, moreover, that we, the public, have no means of knowing how the respective figures on Soviet military strength were arrived at; for this, we are asked to take the word of those same people who are raising the charge of our inferiority and demanding that we move to correct it. In most instances, one must assume, the figures are derived from secret intelligence sources. I see no reason to doubt that good faith of many of those who produce the figures. But we have seen numerous instances in the past (and indeed, we know this to be the tendency in most military establishments) where estimates of the strength of a hypothetical opponent are seriously exaggerated, on the theory that for reasons of prudence one can accept for planning purposes only the most unfavorable to oneself of the various estimates. It would be naïve, furthermore, to pretend that military establishments, in putting out for public and legislative use such figures of another power's strength, are not moved, subconsciously or otherwise, by the reflection that the more frightening the figures appear the greater will be the chances for an authorized increase in their own arsenals.

This does not mean that no confidence at all can be placed in the figures in question. It does mean that the general public, batting entirely in the dark, has to remember that such figures, often representing, as they do, only informed guesses or vague general estimates in the first place, are usually no more than approximate, and tend to reflect a certain bias in favor of the inflation of the strength of any possible opponent.

One notices, finally, that most of these calculations, as they appear in American military-strategic literature, predicate, by implication at least, a totally bipolar world, such as does not actually exist — a world in which there are only the United States and its NATO allies, on the one hand, and the Soviet Union on the other, and each is concerned only with the other's destruction. Neither party, one might conclude, has any other serious military problems to consider than that presented by this one antagonist. Under this view, the respective military establishments have meaning and value only in relation to each other. This is obviously not true; and the error involved in assuming it to be true further vitiates the significance of the figures.

If, in the face of all these facts, one leaves aside for the moment the question of Soviet intentions, and looks at the figures in question only from the standpoint of the comparison of the Soviet and American defense efforts, what emerges with reasonable probability is substantially this: that in recent years the United States, against a background of partial post-Vietnam retrenchment, of heavy inflation in the costs of military hardware, and of virtual sufficiency in certain stocks of weaponry, has materially increased the cost and lowered the pace of its defense preparations, whereas the Soviet Union has continued to press on steadily with its own defense preparations at approximately the rate established in earlier years. The relative weight of the two defense establishments, insofar as it can be measured at all in statistical terms, has thus been somewhat altered to the disadvantage of the United States. This does not mean that the American superiority in most of the significant indicators has been wiped out. Nor is the fact that the Russians may be approaching numerical "equivalence" in a number of respects proof that they intend or expect to go further, once "equivalence" has been achieved, and to seek something called "superiority." All that is only an assumption. The change that has occurred is simply the reflection — not of some new and menacing increase in the rate of development of the Soviet armed forces, but of a temporary diminution, since Vietnam, in the rate of development of our own.

3. THE POLITICAL CHARGE

These figures of comparative military strength are not the only basis for the charge that détente was a failure and that we are now endangered by the conduct of the Soviet government. Closely connected with this, but with a somewhat different focus of emphasis, is the supporting charge that these allegedly menacing defense preparations are only part of a general effort on the part of the Soviet leadership to move out of the position of great and unanswerable regional power which they have so long enjoyed and to challenge the United States for influence and supremacy on a global basis. In support of this thesis it is alleged that the Soviet navy, having long been primarily a defensive instrument designed for the protection of the Soviet coasts and adjacent waters, is now being shaped and readied for an effort at control of the high seas on a global basis. Secondly, the supporters of this thesis point to Soviet involvements in Angola, at other African points (Conakry and Somaliland, particularly, but also with occasional references to Mozambique and Nigeria), and in the Middle East. These involvements, it is suggested, are the expressions of some new and heightened program of overseas expansion, designed to bring all of Africa and the Middle East, and eventually other areas as well, under effective Soviet control.

I find these fears as little convincing as those derived from the comparative figures on weapons production and troop strength.

Take first the question of naval strength. I can do no better than to quote the following passages from the report issued, in November 1976, by the UNA-USA National Policy Panel on Conventional Arms Control, chaired by Messrs. Thornton F. Bradshaw and Cyrus R. Vance:

> . . . the U.S. Navy is a long-range projection force with great staying power. It is clearly a stronger force than the Soviet Navy, despite the larger number of Soviet ships, and the gap may be widening. Recent studies by the Library of Congress have shown that since 1969 the U.S. has constructed 12 per cent more naval vessels than the Soviet Union and the new U.S. ships displace over 70 per cent more tonnage. Moreover, unlike the United States, the Soviet Union has no allies with powerful navies.
>
> By contrast, the Soviet Navy is still largely a denial force, following the traditional pattern of a naval force acting in support of land power. . . . At present the Soviet Union is not capable of projecting naval power long distances if the U.S. chooses to contest such a move.

The report goes on to say that the Soviet navy appears to be undergoing a gradual shift from a "denial" to a "projection" posture, but that this process, if carried to completion, would require an effort of many years. For the moment, furthermore, the report notes (somewhat illogically) that the Soviet naval buildup appears to have leveled off.

All this does not add up to a very menacing pattern. Particularly

[163]

does it fail to suggest any new or drastic decisions in the direction of achieving global supremacy for the Soviet Union.

That there are, in the present composition of the U.S. Navy, disbalances that urgently require correction, that it needs, in particular, a strong capability for providing and protecting logistical support for operations by American forces in Europe, seems beyond question. But this is not a requirement occasioned by any sudden and recent increase in Soviet naval strength or change in evident Soviet plans. It is simply the need for an improvement in our naval posture in the light of our obligations as a member of NATO.

As for the charges that Soviet political activities in Africa and the Near East reflect a major Soviet effort to achieve world domination by the development of political and military footholds in other continents, one can only say the following. The Soviet Union has endeavored for many years to acquire influence with one or another of the factions competing for power in Third World countries. It is an effort not foreign to the practice of great powers generally, including ourselves. What strikes one about these efforts on the Soviet side, particularly in Africa, is not their success but the lack of it.

In Angola, as we have noted, they had what could be seen at best as a stroke of good luck, insofar as the faction they had been supporting for many years suddenly (and probably quite unexpectedly for them) arrived in power. They did indeed pour in heavy infusions of arms at the crucial junction; and presumably they sanctioned, or acquiesced in, the intervention by the Cubans. The curious brief and episodic excursion of South African forces into the Angolan civil war provided them with a convenient excuse for all this. But what surprises is not how much they have done to take advantage, for military and anti-American purposes, of this ostensible good fortune, but how little. There is no evidence that they have developed anything resembling military bases in Angola. They appear to have the occasional use (not control) of an airport there; and there is some reason to suppose that they use it from time to time for aerial reconnaissance purposes in the South Atlantic. Similar arrangements exist, we must suppose, at Conakry, and in Somaliland, at the other side of Africa. There is as yet no evidence of any significant development of Soviet naval or military facilities in Mozambique or in Nigeria.

This very limited use by the Soviet Union of the territory of the Third World countries for military or naval purposes bears no comparison to the similar use made by ourselves in several parts of the world. There is, in particular, nothing comparable to the far-flung network of military and naval bases that the United States has maintained across the world for most of the time since World War II.

To say these things is not to deny that there are disquieting features to Soviet activities of this nature here or there. It *is* to say that these features are, again, not of such a nature as to justify the suggestion that the U.S. and its allies are suddenly in great and new danger; nor do they suggest any new and drastic decisions on the part of the Soviet leadership that would place in question the prospects for a continued peaceful coexistence of the Western community with that country or call for a sudden and drastic increase in U.S. and NATO defense preparations.

Soviet activities in the Near East afford no greater foundation for any such conclusions. There was a time, some years ago, when Soviet activities in that region did indeed have disturbing connotations. It may well be that the Soviet political establishment is still not wholly lacking in persons who would advocate adventuristic courses, strongly hostile and menacing to Western interests, in relation to that part of the world. But there is no evidence that such persons have, today, a decisive influence on Soviet policy. Soviet efforts to bend the countries of the Near East to their uses have, with the partial exception of Iraq and Libya, been signally unsuccessful. There is no reason to suppose that the lessons derived from these disappointments have not been useful. On the contrary, there is evidence that Soviet policies there are considerably more moderate, less ambitious, and less disturbing from the Western standpoint than was the case some years ago. They are not in all respects reassuring; and if we continue to pour arms into Iran in quantities greater than any normal considerations of the defense of that country could warrant, no one can assure that the Soviet leaders will not someday feel their security interests more closely engaged and that this will not affect their policies in ways disagreeable to Western interests. But there is little in their behavior of the recent past (unless it be their threatened action during the Yom Kippur War, the facts of which are still obscure for the general public) to suggest that they have been undergoing a major change of heart of such dimensions as would render their involvement in the affairs of that area more alarming than what we have known in earlier years.

4. Soviet Intentions

On examining these various warnings of heightened Soviet aggressiveness and determination to achieve military superiority, one is struck by certain implicit assumptions that seem to run through them concerning the nature and intentions of the Soviet leadership. These might be summarized as follows:

(a) That the Soviet leadership has not significantly changed since the days of the Cold War and is still primarily inspired by a desire, and intention, to achieve world domination.

(b) That the Soviet leadership views a military showdown with the United States as the inevitable outcome of the ideological and political conflict between the two powers, and looks only for an opportunity to attack the United States and its NATO allies successfully, or to confront them with such overpowering military force that they will "surrender" and place themselves in its power.

(c) That for this reason, the Soviet armed forces serve, in the eyes of the leaders, primarily aggressive rather than defensive purposes.

Supplementing these views there seems to be an assumption on the part of the spokesmen of this thesis, themselves, that the differences of aim and outlook between the Soviet Union and the United States are indeed of such a nature that no peaceful resolution of them is conceivable — that they can be resolved only by war or by the achievement of an unanswerable military superiority by the one party or the other.

I hope to be able, in the following chapter, to treat this question of Soviet intentions at greater length and more adequately. But there are one or two things about these assumptions that ought to be said at this point.

First: When people suggest or imply that there is no significant difference between the Soviet Union we knew at the close of the Stalin era, a quarter of a century ago, and that which we have before us today, this is a sign that those same people have not looked very attentively or deeply at either the composition or the situation of the Soviet regime. Actually, even Stalin, in his final years, seems to have accepted the inevitability, or probability, of an eventual military showdown not because he himself wanted it or thought it necessary from the Soviet standpoint, but rather because he thought the Western powers were determined to push things to that point. But whatever he may then have thought, there is no reason to suppose that the present leadership would see things precisely as he did.

Certainly, if all this could be achieved bloodlessly, without upsetting repercussions at home and without increased responsibilities for the Soviet Union abroad, the leadership of that country would no doubt be pleased — but only within limits — to see such things as abandonment of the Western position in Berlin, a clear Soviet military ascendancy all the way from the Atlantic to the Chinese frontier, and heightened Soviet prestige the world over. Whether they would really like to see a dismantling of American military power in Western Europe is questionable. But that this leadership would wish to see all this achieved by war, even if this could be done with only a relatively moderate amount of military damage to the Soviet Union,

[167]

is highly doubtful. I must dismiss, as unworthy of serious attention, the suggestion that the Soviet leaders would be prepared to accept a loss of several tens of millions of the Soviet population in a nuclear encounter if it could thereby expect to establish a military superiority over the United States. The memories and trauma of World War II are far more active in Russia than people in the West seem generally to realize. Wars, particularly ones waged at distance from the center of Russian power and for purposes that did not seem to include the defense of the heartland, have always been politically dangerous in modern times to Russian governments. And there are other, more subjective reasons for such hesitations on the part of the present leadership, which it will be more useful to treat in the next chapter.

But beyond this, the people who profess to see some sort of a military showdown as inevitable, allegedly because the Soviet leaders are determined to have it, seem themselves to be only too ready to accept that same thesis for themselves, as something flowing from the logic of the conflict of aims and ideals between the two countries. This is perhaps the most dangerous of all the elements in their thinking. For competitive military preparations, pursued over a long period of time, conduce insensibly to the assumption that a military conflict so long and intensively prepared for must at some point take place. People tend, then, to forget that perhaps there was nothing in the actual interests and needs of the respective peoples to justify a war in the first place.

Bismarck, in the final years of his active life, had to contend with just this problem in the tendency of the German military leaders, and many senior political officials in his country, to regard a German-Russian war as inevitable just because the elaborate preparations of the military establishments on both sides of the line made it appear so. In vain, he pleaded with people to understand that Germany had no objectives with regard to Russia that were worth the sacrifices of a war — that war would bring disaster to both parties — such disaster that at the end of it people would no longer even remember the relatively trivial bones of contention out of which it had arisen.

And so it is, today. There is no political or ideological difference between the Soviet Union and the United States — nothing which either side would like, or would hope, to achieve at the expense of the other — that would be worth the risks and sacrifices of a military encounter. Given a realistic appreciation of the limitations of great-power imperialism, and particularly of Russian imperialism, in the modern age, it would be cheaper, safer, and less damaging over the long term for either side to yield on any of the points of difference between them rather than to accept the disaster which modern war would spell. This has been repeatedly demonstrated by recent history. It is evident, for example, that in 1916, in the middle of World War I, either side could have accepted the maximum terms of the other side for ending the war and have been better off than it was by continuing the war for another two years. (To observe this is not to make a plea for political surrender. It is merely to urge that we get our thinking straight.)

While there are no doubt individuals in the Soviet hierarchy of power who do not understand this, there is abundant evidence that the Soviet leadership as a whole does. War, consequently, or even the risk of it that would be implied in any all-out effort to achieve military superiority, is not their favored means of achieving such of their objectives as seem to be in conflict with those of the United States. Nor do any of these objectives, insofar as we can observe them — particularly in Eurasia — seem to be of such a nature as to challenge any vital interest of ours — the only possible exception being Berlin. There appear, however, most unfortunately, to be numbers of Americans to whom none of this is apparent.

It has been noted above that the tendency of the American military mind, when confronted with the argument that the Soviet leaders are perhaps neither determined to do, or even desirous of doing, to us all the dreadful things of which we are now being warned, is to say: "We cannot make assumptions about Soviet intentions. The evidence is too vague and too complex. We must assume them desirous of doing anything injurious to us which they have the capability of doing."

Does it never occur to these people, one wonders, that in taking that position they are themselves making a sweeping assumption about Soviet intentions — namely, the most extreme, most pessimistic, least sophisticated, and most improbable assumption they could make — the assumption, namely, that these, their political opponents, lack all the normal attributes of humanity and are motivated by nothing but the most blind and single-minded urge of destruction towards the peoples and substance of the United States and its allies?

This effort at the dehumanization of the opponent — the insistence on seeing him as the embodiment of all evil, unaffected by motives other than the desire to wreak injury upon others — has bedeviled the leaders of American opinion in two world wars. There should be no place for it in the assessment of another great power in peacetime, and particularly not of one with whom our political differences are not such as to require or justify a war for their settlement. Particularly should there be no place for it in an age when war between great nuclear-armed powers has become mortally dangerous to all participants — as well as nonparticipants.

If the United States is to behave, in the face of the problem of Soviet power, in a manner conducive to its own present security and that of future generations, it has no choice but to put this sort of childishness behind it and consent to look at that power soberly and carefully, for what it is, not for what would fit best into the dialectics of theoretical military planning.

5. Conclusions

To me, the above considerations not only suggest but conclusively demonstrate that the general thesis of a new and heightened danger to this country from recent Soviet military preparations is not supported by the available evidence and has to be rejected as the basis for a useful discussion of the problem now presented to American policy-makers by the phenomenon of Soviet power.

This does not mean that there is no problem at all. It also does not mean that no improvement or strengthening is in order anywhere in the American defense posture. Just as certain adjustments no doubt need to be made in the composition and deployment of American naval strength, so it is entirely possible, even probable, that there is need for changes in the ground force dispositions of NATO in Europe, as is being argued from certain elements on the military side, with a view to reducing their vulnerability to sudden attack, improving their logistical support, and so on. It is perfectly possible that a proper posture for these NATO conventional forces would require further strengthening in one way or another; and the considerations set forth above are not intended as an argument against anything of that sort, where the situation really warrants it. Obviously, the NATO aerial and ground force establishment in Western Europe plays a stabilizing political role; it should not be unilaterally dismantled or seriously weakened; and where strengthening is really needed to assure its suitability to the role it is asked to play, that strengthening should be given.

But there is no reason for persuading oneself that such strengthening, or the strengthening of the strategic nuclear "deterrent," is necessitated by changes in Soviet political and military intensions for which there is no adequate evidence. There is, in fact, the weightiest of reasons for not doing just that; because history has proved that the exaggeration of an adversary's negative attributes, including the evilness of his intentions and the strength he possesses for realizing those supposedly evil intentions, takes on the quality of a self-fulfilling prophecy and tends to promote the arrival of the very dangers it attempts to portray. We have serious enough problems in world affairs today without convincing ourselves of the existence of ones we do not really have.

XII

The Soviet Union—The Reality

LET US SEE WHETHER WE CAN DESCRIBE THE PROBLEM WHICH THE
Soviet Union does present for American policy-makers in these
years of the late 1970s.

1. "WORLD DOMINATION"

"Well, their objectives haven't changed, have they? Don't they still
want to achieve world domination?"

This question must have been asked me hundreds of times in
recent years.

When, in late 1917, Lenin and his associates came to power in
Russia, they did indeed have dreams of early world revolution, in
the sense of the revolutionary overthrow of the great capitalist powers of Western Europe, as a consequence of which, it was thought,
the European colonial empires would be destroyed and the road
opened for the advance of the liberated colonial peoples to economic

development under Communist encouragement and leadership. (Whether the United States originally figured in their view of the world as a major capitalist-imperialist power is uncertain. In any case, it soon came to do so.)

These hopes were based on the enormous agony, spiritual and economic, in which European society had become embraced by that fourth year of World War I. This had bred much unrest and even desperation. Masses of people were embittered by the horrible and senseless slaughter. Empires were tottering. Class structures were being undermined. It seemed, from the viewpoint of those who had seized power in Petrograd, that the prospects for revolution in the remainder of Europe were bright. And they did indeed propose to do whatever they could to promote it.

This did not mean that these early Russian Communist leaders proposed to bring revolution about elsewhere solely by the action of whatever armed forces they could assemble in Russia — to bring it about, that is, by invading other countries and imposing Communist regimes upon reluctant peoples. There was a difference between revolution and conquest. Revolution, as they saw it, was something bound to flow primarily from the action of the indigenous revolutionary proletariat in each country. Revolutionary Russia might give to these proletarian forces in other countries such fraternal assistance — moral, material and military — as it lay within their power to give. But it was never conceived that this assistance should replace revolutionary action by the indigenous proletariat of the countries in question. The role of Russian communism was to assist world revolution, not to create it. The thundering predictions of Lenin — and, later, Stalin — about the inevitability of a final apocalyptic conflict between capitalism and revolutionary socialism, much as they may have suggested to Western minds some sort of final armed struggle between a Communist Russia and the entirety of the non-Communist world, had to be understood in this sense.

Actually, it took no more than three or four years for the leaders of the new Communist regime in Russia to recognize that world revolution, as they had conceived it, was not imminent — that the prospect of it had to be relegated to a future too remote to enter in to serious political planning. Nor did they ever really intend to sacrifice their hard-won power in Russia to a quixotic effort to hasten the course of history in this respect. Lenin had once said, to be sure, that if there were a real chance of revolution in Germany, Communist Russia ought to sacrifice itself to bring this about. But this predicated, first of all, a *real* chance of revolution in Germany; and secondly, as time went on and the civil war ran its course in Russia, it became less and less realistic to speak about sacrificing, for the benefit of Communists elsewhere, positions of power won with so much effort and heroism. By 1921 the preservation and development of Communist power within Russia had clearly become the supreme task of the regime. It was to remain that way for a half century into the future.

The rhetoric of "world revolution" remained, of course. It was basic to the ideology. The thought of the universal triumph of the Marxist outlook, with its obvious political connotations, remained the millennial hope, without which no secular religion (which was what Russian communism really represented) could exist. But it ceased to figure as a serious, immediate goal of policy. From this time on, defensive considerations, flowing from Russia's relative weakness and vulnerability and related not just to the protection of Russia as a country, but also to the protection of the regime vis-à-vis the rest of Russia, were to prevail over aggressive-revolutionary impulses in the minds of those who commanded the destinies of that country.

The Second World War brought significant changes. On the one hand, the spectacle of one great Communist power having to fight side by side with various capitalist powers against another capitalist power further undermined the dream of the final conflict between communism and capitalism. On the other hand, the sudden collapse of both German and Japanese power at the close of the war created unprecedented opportunities for the establishment of the power of the Russian state over large contiguous areas where the recent domination by the Germans and the Japanese had destroyed or decisively weakened indigenous powers of resistance. On all this Stalin capitalized to the best of his ability; and the result was of course the creation of the satellite area of Eastern and Central Europe. This, however, while masked as a gain for "communism," was in reality a revival of traditional Russian power in that region — a nationalist gain rather than an ideological one in the original sense. It represented the satisfaction of regional, rather than global, ambitions on the part of the Stalinist leadership. Furthermore, while it did indeed come to constitute a new military threat to Western Europe, in the sense that the establishment of a Russian bridgehead in the very center of Europe represented a fundamental displacement of the military balance of the continent, it also created new aspects of vulnerability for the Soviet Union itself and served to heighten, rather than to diminish, the weight of defensive considerations in the total pattern of Soviet strategic-political thought.

At the same time, a whole series of postwar phenomena — the consolidation of non-Communist power in the remainder of Europe; the advance of moderate socialism or welfare-state practices in the northern part of that continent; and the success of dissident Communist forces in Yugoslavia and China — further undermined the dream of eventual world revolution under Russian-Communist auspices. From now on, the Soviet Union would behave *in the main* as a normal great power, the traditional concerns and ambitions of Russian rulers taking precedence over ideological ones in the minds of the Soviet leaders.

This did not mean that the ideological concepts played no part at all in the conduct of these men, and above all, in their words and political gestures. On the contrary, the very existence of the Chinese rival, constantly hurling at Moscow the charge of betraying true Communist principles, forced Moscow in self-defense to emphasize the rhetoric, and sometimes even to make the gestures, of revolutionary Marxism. But behind this verbal smokescreen, the men in the Kremlin were really acting overwhelmingly, so far as international affairs were concerned, in the tradition of nationalist Russian rulers of earlier periods. Their predominant and decisive concerns ran to the protection of their own rule within Russia, and also to the security of the Russian heartland which served as the indispensable base for their power and with which, for all their ideological preconceptions, they were indissolubly linked by the powerful bonds of national feeling.

It will be said, of course: yes, but dreams of world domination and a persistent tendency to expansion, as characteristics of Russian outlooks and actions, were not new to Russia in the Communist period; they could be observed for centuries in the conduct of Tsarist statesmen. And, it will further be asked, as the Communist leaders come to conform more closely to the traditional patterns of Russian statesmanship, will not the original ideological motives for aggressive policies simply be replaced, then, by the more traditional ones?

The point is a good one, and not to be answered in a word. In the period of the Grand Duchy of Moscow the intolerant religious orthodoxy on which, in part, the grand dukes based their claim to the legitimacy of their power had global implications. It is also true that in both periods of Tsarist history — Muscovite and Petersburg — the Russian state showed a persistent tendency to what might be called border expansion, extending its power, time after time, to new areas contiguous to the existing frontiers.

The first of these phenomena had serious significance only in the Muscovite period. It was comparable to the ideological orthodoxy of the Soviet period, but was equally remote from any possibility of realization. For this reason it was, like its later-day Marxist counterpart, not very important as a guide to action.

The second of the two phenomena — the tendency to border expansion — affected both Muscovite and Petersburg statesmanship, and has indeed manifested itself in the Soviet period as well. (Stalin was highly affected by it.) It thus poses a more serious question. If it

[177]

does not play a prominent part in the motivation of Soviet leaders today, this is a product, one must assume, of the force of circumstances rather than of natural inclination.

In the West, Stalin left Russia saddled with so vast a *glacis* — so vast a protective belt — in the form of the satellite area, and this represented in itself so serious a responsibility and in some ways a burden, that there was not only no strong incentive for his successors to expand it (West Berlin being the major exception), but any such effort would have posed considerable danger. On the Asiatic border, the stalemate in Korea (after 1952) and the anxious vigilance of the Chinese made further expansion impossible except at the risk of a major war. This left only three border regions of any significance: Afghanistan, where, for the moment, the situation was not such as to invite or justify expansionist moves on the Russian side; Iran, where again the risks were higher and the possible profit very small; and finally, the Scandinavian North, where the NATO activity and the naval rivalry indeed provided new defensive incentives for an extension of Russian power but where, again, the NATO involvement meant that any attempt to realize such an extension would involve very high risks of major war.

In these circumstances, the traditional Russian tendency to border expansion has found few promising outlets, and except in Asia — little incentive in recent years. It may make itself felt again in the more distant future. For the moment it is not a major component in Soviet motivation. It is, in any case, an impulse which is regional, not universal, in character.

There is one last facet of Soviet policy that will perhaps be cited as evidence of the alleged desire to achieve "world domination." That is the extent to which Moscow has recently involved itself with the resistance movements of Southern Africa and with leftist political factions in other Third World countries.

I am afraid that I am unable to see in this phenomenon anything that is particularly new, anything that falls outside the normal patterns of great-power behavior, anything that proceeds from purely aggressive, as distinct from defensive, motives, or anything reflecting a belief that there is a serious prospect for a major extension of Soviet power through such involvements.

The effort to assist to the seats of power in distant countries factions whose aims seem reasonably compatible with one's own is, as I have already noted, not foreign to the normal practice of great powers, including the United States. Why it should cause such great surprise or alarm when it proceeds from the Soviet Union I fail to understand. The high degree of responsiveness of African resistance leaders to pseudo-Marxist ideas and methods, justifying as these do both heavy bloodshed as a means to the attainment of power and the establishment of a ruthless dictatorship to assure the maintenance of it, presents a powerful invitation to Soviet involvement and one which, incidentally, they can scarcely reject without playing into the hands of the Chinese critics and rivals. Too often, a failure on the Soviet side to respond to such appeals for support is to throw the respective factions into the arms of the Chinese.

In any case, recent Soviet efforts along this line would appear to have been on a scale hardly comparable to our own, and no greater than those of the Chinese. The Russians have known no Vietnams in recent years. They have not even sent their own forces abroad into other countries (the exception being the Eastern European region which we, by tacit consent, assigned to their good graces in 1945) — a measure of restraint which we Americans can scarcely claim for ourselves. And such efforts as they have made to support factions agreeable to their concepts and purposes in Third World countries do not strike me as exceeding, either in nature or in scale, the efforts their Communist predecessors mounted, without inspiring great alarm in American opinion, in earlier decades.

All in all, then, these apprehensions of a Russian quest for "world domination," which have been used to justify appeals for a totally negative, hostile, and militaristic attitude towards the Soviet Union, have little substance behind them and are not responsive to the real profile of the problem which the existence of Communist power in Russia presents for American statesmanship.

2. THE INTERNAL SITUATION

No Western policy towards the Soviet Union that fails to take into account the nature and situation of the present Soviet leadership can be a sound one. Much of the discussion of Soviet-American relations on the alarmist side is cast in terms indistinguishable from those that were being used at the height of the Cold War, around the time of the death of Stalin. One would suppose, to read this material, that no significant change of any sort had taken place since Stalin's death — that the men now in power presented precisely the same problem from our standpoint as their predecessors of a quarter of a century ago. Actually, this is far from being the case.

The present Soviet leadership is, as governing groups in great countries go, an exceptionally old one. The average age of the top five or six figures is well over seventy. About half the members of the all-powerful Politburo (full and alternate) are upwards of sixty-six years of age. Half the members of the Presidium of the Council of Ministers (the governmental counterpart of the Politburo, which is the supreme *Party* body) are over sixty. The advanced age of the senior leadership in the Soviet Union is a fact well known to all students of Soviet affairs.

This does not mean that the men in question are ineffectual or lacking in the capacity for hard work. It does mean that they are men who have had long and sobering governmental experience. Men of this age and this experience are not normally given to adventuristic policies or to moves likely to impose enormous additional strains and uncertainties upon themselves and upon the system of power they head.

The composition of the Politburo and the other senior bodies of the regime has remained remarkably stable for well over a decade. And this stability has communicated itself to the entire senior bureaucracy — political, military, and economic — a body numbering several hundred people. At the last Congress of the Communist Party, held in March 1976, 90 percent of those elected to the Central Committee, a body in which all the powerful figures of the regime are represented, were being re-elected, which means that they had already belonged to that body for at least five years. Most of them, in fact, had been there longer.

Entry into this senior bureaucracy from lower echelons is, in these circumstances, a rare privilege, and difficult to achieve. Candidates for such promotion are obviously examined with extreme care by the top leadership; and everything known about their personalities suggests that among the qualities that commend them for it are steadiness, balance of view, ability to fit into the bureaucratic machinery, and a quiet loyalty and dependability that does not preclude independent initiative and judgment.

The methods by which these senior echelons of the bureaucracy are kept in line by the top leadership differ radically from those of Stalin. He controlled them by sheer terror and by pitting them one against the other in a struggle for favor where the slightest misstep spelled personal disaster. This assured their slavish obedience but lamed their powers of initiative and their effectiveness as administrators. The present leadership relies on more traditional and conventional means of control: outstandingly the meticulous and judicious distribution of authority, prestige and privilege.

Now a senior bureaucracy chosen and handled in this way is not something that the top leadership can disregard or push around at will. The mutual dependence is too great. It has to be carefully "managed" ("*menagé*," in the French sense). There are limits to the extent to which it can safely be taken unaware by abrupt decisions of the ruling group, or changes of policy for which it would not be prepared and would have no understanding.

I emphasize this, because many of the more alarmist visions of Soviet behavior, as now voiced in the United States, seem to reflect a view of the top Soviet leadership as a group of men who, having all internal problems effectively solved and nothing to do but to plot our destruction, sit at the pinnacle of a structure of power whose blind and unquestioning obedience resembles that of a tremendously disciplined military force, poised for the attack and only awaiting superior orders. This is unrealistic even from the standpoint of the actual relations between that leadership and its own bureaucracy. It is even more unrealistic when applied to the relationship of that leadership with the leaders of the Eastern European satellite regimes. And it disregards another factor commonly regarded in the West as insignificant in the case of Russia, namely: public opinion within the country. Public opinion in Russia naturally does not play the same role in Russia that it plays under a democratic system; but it is not wholly without importance in the eyes of the regime, if only because it affects political and labor morale. The reactions of common people, too, are something the regime has to think about before it launches on abrupt and drastic changes of policy. All this has relevance, of course, to the fears expressed in the West about a sudden Soviet attack on Western Europe, for it affects the ability of the regime to take full advantage of the element of surprise.

The Soviet leadership must be seen, then, as an old and aging group of men, commanding — but also very deeply involved with — a vast and highly stable bureaucracy. This bureaucracy is very much a creature of habit. It is effective in governing the country, but it would not be a very flexible instrument for sudden or abrupt changes. This does not preclude a certain amount of conspiratorial activity on the part of the secret intelligence services and of those sections of the Party which deal with clandestine operations in foreign countries. It does mean that the Soviet apparatus of power is not one that can suddenly be turned around and switched, in the course of a few days, from the normal governing of the country to the huge and wholly abnormal exertions of a major war.

All of the above would be true even if the main concerns of this top leadership were ones addressed primarily to foreign affairs, and specifically to thoughts of aggressive expansion at the expense of other powers. Actually, there is no reason to suppose that this last is the case. The overwhelming weight of evidence indicates that there has never been a time since the aftermath of the recent war when the main concerns of the Soviet leadership have not been ones related to the internal problems that face them: first, the preservation of the security of their own rule within the country, and secondly, the development of the economic strength of a country which, although considerably greater than the United States in area and population, has only roughly one half of the latter's gross national product.

With respect to the first of these concerns the leadership faces a number of problems — not immediately crucial ones, but ones that give it no small measure of puzzlement and anxiety. One of these is the general indifference, among the population, towards the ideological pretensions of the regime, and the curious sort of boredom and spiritlessness that overcome so much of Soviet society in the face of the insistence of the regime that nothing but that same stale and outdated ideology must find expression in either public utterance or organized activity. This has a number of negative consequences which the regime cannot ignore. Not the least of these is the appalling growth of alcoholism in all echelons of the population but particularly among the working youth. Another one is the continuing vitality of religious faith under a regime which has always held religion in contempt and created its own ideology as a replacement for it.

This situation, in which the populace simply does not have at heart, and indeed is indifferent to, what the regime puts forward as the source of its own legitimacy and the sole acceptable motive power for political and social activity, is an unsettling one from the standpoint of the leadership. It finds an even more unsettling counterpart in the state of affairs which prevails throughout the satellite area of Eastern Europe, where lack of interest for the official dogma is even more widespread, more pronounced, and less concealed. In

[183]

normal times, all this can be controlled, and partly concealed, by the usual devices of authoritarian power. But it means that the spiritual and political foundation on which Soviet power rests is not entirely a sound one; there are limits to the weight it could be asked to bear.

Then there is, of course, the problem of dissent among the intellectuals. This is probably not as much of a problem as the American press would have us believe. For the reporters in Moscow, the dissidents are close at hand, and their strivings and sufferings make good copy. Actually, the dissidents have few means of appealing for mass support within the country. And their aims are unfortunately somewhat confused by association in the public mind with the cause of Jewish emigration — a confusion for which the Western press, again, has largely itself to blame. Nevertheless, they present a disturbing problem, particularly for a regime which, unjust as are many of the methods it employs to repress dissidence, is unwilling to return to the wholly ruthless and cruel devices of the Stalin era. The dissidents present a problem whether they are kept at home or permitted to emigrate; and the regime appears to vacillate, with much uncertainty, between the two methods of treatment. While their activities are not a serious immediate threat, no fully satisfactory means has been found of dealing with them. And if, with time, their message begins to get through to student youth and to touch those mysterious springs of student revolt which bubble up so suddenly and seemingly unaccountably in all countries, the danger could become more serious. It was, after all, something very similar to this that occurred in the final decades of the last century and laid much of the groundwork for the eventual demise of the Tsarist regime.

The concerns just mentioned relate to the state of mind of the Soviet population as a whole. But there is a special dimension to this problem in the form of the strong nationalistic feelings that prevail in certain of the non-Russian constituent republics of the Soviet Union. It was the original pretension of the regime that the Marxist-Leninist ideology would provide the fraternal bond which would unite these

peoples with the Russian people and justify their inclusion in the Soviet Union. One of the great tragic problems that has confronted the
Soviet leadership ever since the inception of the Russian-Communist
state has been the fact that in this century national feelings have
shown themselves to be more powerful as a political-emotional force
than ones related, as is the Marxist ideology, to class rather than to
nation. Thus many people in the non-Russian republics who have no
great objection to the concepts and practices of Marxist socialism *per
se* experience a strong restlessness by virtue of the subjugation to
Russian rule which — to them — their inclusion in the Soviet
Union implies. This is aggravated by the fact that in some instances
these people have a stronger tradition of individualism generally and
of private economic initiative in particular than have the Russians.
And its seriousness as a problem for the Soviet leadership is further
heightened by the fact that in certain of these republics the population is increasing faster than in Russia proper, so that the balance between Russians and non-Russians in the Soviet Union, already one
of approximately half and half, is steadily changing to the disadvantage of the Russian inhabitants of the central heartland.

Like the problem of the dissidents, this national restlessness in the
constituent republics is not a serious short-term problem for the
regime, but it is a hard one to cope with; for both tolerance and
repression tend to enhance rather than to dispel it. If, therefore, the
regime does not have to fear it excessively in the short term, it has to
recognize that it has still not found the answer to it. And this, too, is
disturbing for anyone within the regime who has any historical
sense; because the very similar nationalistic restlessness that prevailed among certain of these minority peoples in the Tsarist time
proved, when that regime came under severe pressure, to be one of
the major factors that conduced to its downfall.

Added to these concerns, and probably more important than any
of them in the claims they place on the attention of the leaders, are
the various continuing problems of the economic development of the
country. An enormous amount has been achieved in this respect in

recent decades; but there are still problem areas which give rise to serious concern. Chief among these, of course, is the persistent inadequacy of Soviet agriculture to meet the needs of a growing population. This is not all the fault of the mistakes of collectivization; some of it can be traced to the unfortunate oddities of climate and geography with which Soviet agriculture is plagued. But whatever the causes, it is a situation which has not ceased to be a source of grave anxiety to those charged with the task of making the Soviet system work. And beyond this, there are the other problems: technological backwardness (in comparison with the advanced West) in a number of key areas; the inability of the system to create a distribution system for consumer goods that compares with that of Western countries; shortage of proper housing; and the continuing relative inefficiency of labor.

All these factors deserve attention, because they mean that even if the Soviet leaders had wistful ideas of pressing for some sort of a military contest or showdown with the West, they would not wish to proceed in this direction, or even to hasten the arrival of such a situation, until they had progressed much farther than is the case today in the overcoming of these various inadequacies, inefficiencies, and elements of political vulnerability in the situation at home.

3. The External Situation

Just as the security (not the expansion) of their own power is the prime consideration for the Soviet leaders when they face their own country, so it is when they face the outside world.

This means for them, first of all, no premature or unsettling relaxation of Soviet authority over the Eastern European satellite area. The Soviet leadership could possibly accommodate itself, in time, to a greater degree of independence on the part of one or another of the countries concerned (to a certain extent it has already done so), but only if this does not change the military-political balance in Europe in a manner too detrimental to Soviet military security or prestige, and only if it does not set up liberationist ripples that would carry into the Soviet Union itself. This last is a greater danger than it would have been before 1939, because the extension of the Soviet borders so far to the west during World War II had the effect of bringing into the Soviet Union peoples who are more sensitive to happenings elsewhere in Eastern and Central Europe than are the Russians themselves.

The first requirement of Soviet foreign policy is thus the preservation of the present delicate balance of forces in Europe and, in the absence of any satisfactory arrangements with the Western powers for mutual disengagement or withdrawal in Central Europe, the assurance of the integrity of Soviet hegemony in that region. This, the reader will note, is a strongly defensive consideration.

The second requirement, not addressed to relations with "capitalist" countries, but one which nevertheless belongs in the category of foreign policy, is the protection of the image of the Soviet Union as the central bastion of revolutionary socialism throughout the world, and of the Soviet Party leadership as a uniquely wise and prestigious body of men, endowed with a profound understanding of Marxist principles and enjoying great experience in their application — hence, an indispensable source of guidance for Communist and national-liberationist forces everywhere.

This, obviously, is the ideal, not the complete present-day reality. It is an ideal which has been steadily eroded in recent years, and is still under severe attack by the Chinese and others. But it is not wholly devoid of political substance. It is the pretense, if not the reality, and it must, in the eyes of the men in the Kremlin, be defended at all costs.

Why defended? Because the forfeiture or serious undermining of this image would spell for the leadership the most dangerous sort of isolation and insecurity: isolation between a capitalist world which has not fully accepted it, and could not fully accept it, and a Communist world that had lost confidence in it and rejected it; insecurity, because the loss of this image would throw into question the legitimacy of the regime at home. The posture of moral and political ascendancy among the Marxist and national-liberationist political forces of the world is essential to the justification of the dictatorship exercised over, and the sacrifices demanded of, the peoples of the soviet Union for more than half a century. Having once forfeited the plausibility of this external posture, it would be hard to maintain the internal one.

This is a situation which will be fully comprehensible, perhaps, only to those who have some idea of the importance that attaches to theory and pretense in the Russian scheme of things — an importance which normally looms greater in Russian eyes than that of the underlying reality. This, in any case, is the reason why the leaders of the Soviet Union could not possibly consider the abandonment of the role of a principled, dedicated force — the leading force, in fact — for the implementation of the ideals of Marxist socialism, and why they cannot do other than to try to protect themselves, by a vigorous show of orthodox Communist verbiage and activity directed to the Third World, against the attacks of the Chinese and other dissident Communist forces, aimed precisely at the image they feel obliged to preserve.

This motivation underlies a multitude of facets of Soviet behavior with relation to the countries of the Third World. It is not the only motivation that affects that behavior. Military and economic considerations also enter in. But it is the primary source of most of those Soviet policies and actions with relation to the southern continents that arouse so much indignation and alarm in Washington.

The danger that would be presented for the Soviet leadership by the loss of importance as the center of the Communist world is not just a political and psychological one. It also has military-strategic implications of the gravest nature. The loss of this position, as we have just seen, would mean that Soviet Russia would fall between two chairs: between a Communist world that had rejected it and a capitalist world that would not accept it. And it just happens that the outstanding powers of each of these two forces, the dissident Communist world and the distasteful capitalist one, are also, as things stand today, the powers that pose the greatest military threats to the Soviet Union: China and the United States. The loss of the image of leadership among the Communist forces of the world would thus subject the Soviet Union to a military isolation as well as a political one.

We have noted the way in which Soviet military power appears to people in the United States. How does American military power, in conjunction with other NATO power, appear to the people in the Kremlin?

Let us remember, first of all, that since the Korean War the Soviet Union has been faced with an American-NATO defense establishment which was in most respects superior to its own. It has been superior, above all, in nuclear strategic power, and still is. It has had a superiority in warheads and in missile accuracy. It has had a superior strategic bombing arm. It has ringed the Soviet Union with missile bases: in Western Europe, in Greece and Turkey, in Okinawa and Korea, and I don't know where else. It has had, particularly when the navies of the European NATO powers were included, a clear naval superiority. Only in ground force strength in Central Europe could it be considered inferior to that which the Soviet Union has been able to mobilize against it — and even there, not as much as is commonly alleged.

This is the way things really have been. But let it also be remembered that the way things are is not always the way they appear. There is no reason to doubt that not only do the Soviet strategists not exaggerate the strength of their own power as we do, but they probably do exaggerate, conversely, the strength of ours. The picture I have just painted has to be magnified to some undetermined but surely not insignificant extent to take account of this distortion. I am not sure that even in Central Europe the balance of forces looks to the Russians so overwhelmingly favorable to them as we suppose. The weaknesses of the satellite forces are better known to them than to us, and no doubt loom larger in their scheme of things. And I see no reason to suppose that twenty-nine NATO divisions, eleven of them armored and several of them German, supported with nearly seven thousand of so-called tactical nuclear weapons, look to them like the pitiable and hopelessly inferior force they are constantly depicted as being to the Western European and American public. Particularly would this be the case if the strength of the Warsaw Pact forces should be actually, as I suspect, substantially that which the Communist negotiators recently revealed, for the first time, to their opposite numbers in the talks on the Mutual and Balanced Force Reductions. The Western negotiators, who had long demanded these figures, received them with scornful skepticism when they were finally made available. But are we so sure that the error was not in our own exaggerations?

To this it will be said, I know, that all this cannot be a source of serious concern to them, for they know that our intentions are good. Really?

Let us remember that here, too, as in the military field, there is a distortion of the lenses that makes a capitalist government appear — insists, in fact, that it must be — hostile and menacing in its intentions towards the bastion of world communism. This thesis has been carried forward in a myriad of forms by the Soviet propaganda apparatus for a quarter of a century. It is not to be expected that it has had no place at all in the thinking of the Soviet leaders. The extent to which they believe their own propaganda is always a question; the one thing that is fairly certain is that they always believe it *to some extent*.

But beyond this, the Soviet leaders are all aware that there are forces operating in American political society, as in that of some of the Western European countries, which are bitterly and actively hostile to them and would not be in the least averse to the use of military measures against them, if there were the slightest prospect of success. They have not forgotten the Captive Nations Resolution, still on the books, which commits the legislative branch of the United States government to the overthrow of Communist power everywhere in Russia and Eastern Europe. They never forget that the strongest continental component of NATO is a Western Germany harboring millions of people whom they, the Russians, threw out of their homes — a Western Germany where these refugees and millions of nonrefugees greatly resent the division of the country, and resent particularly the measures that have been taken (outstandingly the Berlin Wall) to try to guard Eastern Germany from the insidious effects of Western influence. The fact that these measures were the expression of a consciousness of great political weakness on the Communist side makes things no better from the Soviet standpoint; on the contrary, it increases the sense of insecurity they experience when they try to translate political realities into military terms. Finally, they remember vividly what most Western Europeans seem to have forgotten: that it was not so long ago that a united Germany — a Germany only a third stronger, let us say, than the Western Germany that exists today — was able to wreak vast destruction in their country and to penetrate all the way to the Volga and the North Caucasus while holding off, at the same time, the combined forces of France and England in the West. Are they, then, to minimize the potential power of the western two-thirds of Germany when it is not opposed to but *in association with* not only the forces of a number of other Western European countries including France and Britain but also those of the United States? To understand the reactions of the Russians, we must credit them with a much longer memory than that of the Western press, and one that does not make light of potential German power.

It may be argued that the Russians should not let themselves be put off by the existence of forces militantly hostile to them in Western societies — that they should look more calmly and deeply at the balance of political forces in the West, from which scrutiny they could confirm that the extremists have never carried the day, that the weight of Western opinion remains strongly opposed to the idea of another war, and that there has never been a time when the NATO governments, collectively or individually, have been disposed to initiate a war against them. All this is true. But the reproach to the Russians for not looking at things this way would come with better grace from a Western community that was prepared to look in the same way at Russia — and to observe the same things in the pattern of Soviet political behavior.

All this is said simply to make the point that the Soviet view of the military balance, and of Western capabilities and intentions, is not the same as ours, and that they do not view with complacency the great accumulation of armed men and weaponry arrayed against them, inadequate as this accumulation may appear to many of us.

I have no means of knowing exactly how the Soviet leaders rate the military strength of Communist China, as it faces them across the long Siberian border. I know only that they rate it highly enough to compel them (if the figures obviously emanating from American intelligence sources are to be believed) to keep on that frontier a huge military force: something in the neighborhood of forty to forty-five divisions and close to a million men.

This is a fact of overwhelming strategic significance. How anyone could overlook its obvious implications I fail to understand. For many decades, a standard feature of Russian strategic thinking, Tsarist and Soviet, has been the determination to avoid, if in any way possible, a two-front war that would require the splitting of the Soviet armed forces between the European and Far Eastern theaters. One does not need to be a Russian to feel the force of this consideration. The military planners of any great country would react the same way.

Apprehension about the Chinese threat is heightened by the extreme vulnerability of the long Russian line of communications along the southern border of Siberia to the Pacific. Exposed for thousands of miles to flank attacks from the south, squeezed in perilously at one point between the Mongolian border and Lake Baikal, this line of communication presents a tremendous problem for Soviet military planners.

Apprehension is further sharpened by the very high degree of tension and emotionalism that marks both sides of this most curious relationship and could cause minor incidents to blaze up into major onces with great rapidity.

In the face of this pattern of fact, the fears voiced in this country and in Western Europe about the present danger of a surprise Soviet attack against the NATO countries of Western Europe are almost too bizarre to be credible. Aside from all the other evidence that the Soviet leaders have neither the incentive nor the capacity to launch this sort of attack in that region, the situation on the Chinese border would alone be more than enough to preclude all thought of anything of this sort. How, one wonders, do those who bandy these alarmist fantasies picture the Soviet leaders? Do they see them as utterly devoid of any sense of political and strategic realism, or as men who, for some unexplained reason, have taken leave of their senses entirely? It would have to be one or the other.

The present tension between the Soviet Union and China, it may be argued, cannot be counted on to last forever. The quarrel may be composed. Then the Kremlin would be free to pursue its supposed desire to unleash a new world war.

Nothing (as one high Soviet official once observed to me) is impossible, in politics. But some things are improbable, even highly so; and one of them is an early resolution of the Soviet-Chinese conflict — a resolution, that is, of so far-reaching a character that the Soviet government could afford to withdraw the forces it now maintains on the Chinese border and to throw itself into a military action against the West, secure in the confidence that the Chinese would view this action benevolently and would refrain from taking advantage of it. A superficial rapprochement between Moscow and Peking, involving agreements on border problems and trade and accompanied by a number of amicable gestures and polite words, is not at all beyond the realm of early possibility. But the creation of an atmosphere of complete confidence, based on a general mutual understanding with regard to world problems and a consciousness of far-reaching identity of political interests, is something that could scarcely be achieved in anything less than many years, perhaps decades, if indeed it could ever be achieved at all.

The fact is that the interests of these two great countries *do* differ materially in important respects. And the habits of extreme secrecy of deliberation, plus an exaggerated sensitivity in matters of internal security, to all of which both parties are addicted, militate against the early achievement of any firm and reliable understanding between them. A wise Western diplomacy neither will count on the prospect of a Soviet-Chinese war nor will it take fright if Chinese and Soviet representatives begin at some point to say amiable things and to toast each other at banquets. There are deeper and more durable elements involved in this relationship — ones which militate, for both parties, against the costly adventure of major war but also make it virtually unthinkable, now and for many years to come, that either should relax its guard. So long as things are this way, those Western alarmists who try to persuade us that a surprise Soviet attack against Western Europe is a serious possibility, unless we vastly increase our power to deter it, are living in a dream world of their own and are talking about a Soviet leadership many of the rest of us have never heard of.

When the Soviet leaders look eastward, it is not only China they see. They also see Japan, and are well aware of its immense importance. They would like, of course, to assure against too close an association, particularly in the military field, between Japan and China. Even the American presence in the area is preferable, in their view, to *that*. They are also eager to obtain, and have in part obtained, Japanese assistance in the development of the resources of the Soviet Far East.

There are, however, two formidable obstacles to any far-reaching further development of Soviet-Japanese relations. One is an intangible: the curious emotional preference on the part of the Japanese, built partly of guilt complex, partly of cultural admiration, for the Chinese over the Russians. The second, more specific, is the question of the four southernmost islands of the chain stretching from the Japanese Hokkaido to Kamchatka — islands that the Russians profess to see as belonging to the Kuriles, which are under their control, whereas the Japanese see them as properly a part of Japan.

Moscow could no doubt appreciably improve its relations with Japan were it able to yield on this point. But there is apparently a fear on the part of the leadership that to do so would be to make itself vulnerable to similar demands for readjustment of borders in Europe, where the Soviet Union also appropriated to itself several areas which other governments do not regard as historically or otherwise natural parts of Russia and would like to recover. Particularly sensitive, in this respect, are territories of Bessarabia, where the likely claimant for restitution would be the Communist government of Rumania, and the erstwhile purely German province of East Prussia, half on which was taken by the Soviet Union in 1945 and the fate of which would be of interest to Eastern as well as to Western Germany. In its relations with Japan, Moscow is hung up, actually, on the consequences of Stalin's greedy thirst for more territory at the end of the last war. Thus, even in international politics, are the sins of the father visited upon the sons.

In present circumstances, given the relatively minor strength and defensive posture of the Japanese armed forces as well as the close association of Japan with the United States, the Moscow leadership can view its relations with that country with a sort of wary acceptance, if not satisfaction. But it is also aware of the potentially explosive quality of the situation in Korea, and knows that a renewed military conflict between the two Korean regimes on that peninsula could produce incalculable complications, involving China, the United States, and Japan, as well as itself.

This, too, the men in the Kremlin have to have in mind when

they design their policies towards the United States and the West. They have to recognize that a major war between Soviet Russia and the NATO alliance would in all probability blow this delicate situation in and around Korea sky-high and have consequences, at present unforeseeable, which could affect Soviet security in the most intimate way.

Then there is, of course, the Near and Middle East.

This is, let us first remember, a region much closer to the Soviet borders than it is to ours. It would be idle to expect the Soviet leaders not to feel their interests seriously affected by whatever happens in that area.

On the other hand, it should also be recognized that, as noted above, they have no active political interests in that area — none, that is, other than those dictated by the strictest considerations of their own national defense — that could conceivably be worth the predictable disasters of a war with the United States. This being the case, they have a vital interest, as we should have, in seeing to it that the internal conflicts of the area do not take forms that would set the two superpowers at war.

In view of the high sensitivity of this region from the standpoint of their military interests, the Soviet leaders would obviously like to have a maximum of influence there, and have tried their best to acquire it. The methods they adopted were not always wise, and have not always been successful. On the contrary, they must, today, feel a very strong sense of disillusionment and frustration as they turn their eyes in that direction. And these feelings must be supplemented with a new element of alarm as they sit by and watch the pouring of these unconscionable quantities of American weaponry into Saudi Arabia and, more disturbing still, into the neighboring Iran. The United States government can consider itself lucky that the Soviet leadership has shown such patience as it has in the face of this reckless procedure, and that it has preferred to wait, and to keep its options open, rather than to move actively to oppose it, as we did in the case of Cuba. But this patience cannot be counted on to endure indefinitely, unless reassurance can be found in the form of some general understanding with the United States with respect to the area in general.

Soviet policy in regard to the Arab-Israeli conflict has obviously been the product of strong differences of opinion within the Moscow political establishment. There would appear to have been those who would not have hesitated to see Israel sacrificed to the cause of a closer Arab-Soviet relationship, if the latter could be obtained this way; and there have been times when, in specific decisions, it looked as though these people had carried the day. At best, it may be said that their influence was sufficient to occasion considerable vacillation and confusion in Soviet policy. But by and large, one has the impression that the Soviet leaders have realized, increasingly, that the destruction of the state of Israel would not only put an end to what is left of their influence with the Arabs but would probably produce a degree of instability in the affairs of the region, not to mention increased involvement of the United States, which could just as easily imperil Soviet interests as serve them.

Such being the case, one must assume that the Soviet leaders would not be disinclined, today, to reach an understanding with the United States and others over the affairs of the region, if this would help to assure that it would not be exploited against them by any other great power and would reinforce the security of their sensitive southern border.

The Soviet leaders view Western Europe, we may be sure, with a troubled and unhappy eye. Its intimate military association with the United States has always been disturbing. Its high living standards provide an uncomfortable comparison with the gray and depressed quality of personal life in so much of Eastern Europe. The lurid quality of its fleshpots and recreations — its very decadence, in fact — tends to unsettle Communist youth, to the extent they are able to learn about it. And the proximity to power of the French and

[197]

Italian Communist parties is, as we have seen, a decidedly dubious phenomenon from the Soviet standpoint. The failures of those parties are apt to stand as the failures of Communism generally in world opinion; whereas their successes, bound to increase their independence, can serve only to diminish Russian authority in the world Communist movement and to increase the size of the already large sector of it that goes its own way.

Well aware that extensive disarray in Western Europe could and probably would mean similar disarray in Eastern Europe, the men in the Kremlin have no desire to see the stability of the situation there severely disrupted. In these circumstances, NATO and the Common Market probably stand out as lesser evils than the visible alternatives, although they cannot say so. Least of all would these men like to see the whole European continent plunged into the extreme and utterly incalculable chaos of a major war. The one thing that would be certain would be that the status quo that emerged from such a war, even in Eastern Europe, would scarcely resemble that which had existed before, even for that portion of the European population that might have survived the holocaust. What ensued might, from the Soviet standpoint, be worse; it is hard to conceive that it could be much better.

Eastern Germany remains, for various reasons, the kingpin of the entire Soviet position in Eastern and Central Europe. For this reason, Moscow is obliged to cling to positions, with relation to Berlin, to the Wall, and to the division of Germany generally, that are bound to stand as impediments to any fully satisfactory relationship to Western Germany and to Western Europe. Many of the individual stances and reactions this necessitates are ones that must inevitably be irritating and unacceptable to Western opinion and a burden on Soviet-German relations in particular. They accept this. It should not be confused with a desire on their part to throw Western Europe and much of the rest of the world into turmoil unimaginable by unleashing a new world war. This would be true even if the nuclear deterrent, strategic or tactical, did not exist at all.

The above observations have dealt with the Soviet view of the situations prevailing in those geographic areas that are of greatest importance to the Soviet Union. There remain, of course, the many and constantly changing problems of the Third World. Here, political necessity obliges Moscow to try to keep its hand in as a supportive force for left-wing and national-liberationist efforts of every sort. But the opportunities, these days, are few. So far has the cause of anticolonialism advanced that there are not many more worlds to be conquered in the way of posing as the noble protector of downtrodden peoples struggling for emancipation from the yoke of the colonialists. Aside from one or two places, such as Chile, where there are indigenous regimes that can be opposed on old-fashioned ideological grounds, there is not much left but the resistance movements directed to the overthrow of white rule in Southern Africa. These, in the circumstances, Moscow must be expected to make the best of. The effort is unfortunate, and not to be taken lightly. It contributes, of course, to what may well be an appalling amount of bloodshed and tragedy throughout that entire region. That it will lead to any sort of effective Soviet hegemony over the nonwhite peoples of the area when and if they have achieved the slaughter or expulsion of the whites is not, however, to be expected; and it is improbable that Moscow itself expects it. It is doing there what it feels, in the face of the Chinese challenge, it has no choice but to do. Whether it enjoys the experience, or hopes for much to come of it in the way of positive political achievement, is doubtful.

4. Summary

If these considerations have any validity, the position of the Soviet leadership might be summed up somewhat as follows:

This is an aging, highly experienced, and very steady leadership, itself not given to rash or adventuristic policies. It commands, and is deeply involved with, a structure of power, and particularly a higher bureaucracy, that would not easily lend itself to the implementation of policies of that nature. It faces serious internal problems, which constitute its main preoccupation.

As this leadership looks abroad, it sees more dangers than inviting opportunities. Its reactions and purposes are therefore much more defensive than aggressive. It has no desire for any major war, least of all for a nuclear one. It fears and respects American military power even as it tries to match it, and hopes to avoid a conflict with it. Plotting an attack on Western Europe would be, in the circumstances, the last thing that would come into its head.

The most active external concerns of this leadership relate, today, to the challenge to its position within the world Communist movement now being mounted by the Chinese and others. It will consider itself fortunate if, in the face of this challenge, it succeeds in preserving its pre-eminence within the Communist sector of the world's political spectrum, in avoiding a major war which, as it clearly recognizes, would be the ruin of everyone involved, itself included, and in ending its own days peacefully — its members going down in history as constructive leaders who contributed, much more than Stalin and at least as much as Khrushchev, to the advancement of the glory of the Soviet Union and the cause of world communism.

XIII

======

Soviet-American Relations

THE IMPLICATIONS FOR AMERICAN FOREIGN POLICY OF WHAT I HAVE
said are probably already apparent in their broader outlines; but I
shall summarize them, as briefly as I can.

1. THE MILITARY DANGER

Let us, first of all, divest ourselves of the widespread fixation that
our differences with the Russians must someday end in war — or
that military strength, in any case, must be the ultimate arbiter of
them. A war between the two countries is not inevitable. The Soviet
leaders themselves, and outstandingly Brezhnev personally, do not
want it. There is nothing in the divergent political interests of the
two countries to necessitate or justify it.

If we insist on placing military considerations at the heart of our
consideration and discussion of Soviet-American relations, we run a
strong risk of eventually bringing about the very war we do not want
and should be concerned to avoid. History shows that belief in the

inevitability of war with a given power affects behavior in such a way as to cripple all constructive policy approaches towards that power, leaves the field open for military compulsions, and thus easily takes on the character of a self-fulfilling prophecy. A war regarded as inevitable or even probable, and therefore much prepared for, has a very good chance of eventually being fought.

Let us teach ourselves to look at the Soviet problem as a serious political one which has, indeed, military implications, but to bear in mind that these implications are of a secondary, not primary, nature; and let us not be hypnotized by military values to the point where we become blind to the others and fail to develop the hopeful and constructive possibilities of the relationship.

The greatest danger inherent in the existing competition between the Soviet Union and the United States in the military field is not the danger of a Soviet attack on ourselves or on NATO; it is the danger that the momentum of this tremendous and infinitely dangerous weapons race will get out of hand, will become wholly uncontrollable, and will, either through proliferation or by accident, carry us all to destruction. Even as things stand today, the sheer volume — the megatonnage — of nuclear explosives in our hands and in those of our Soviet adversaries is a menace to all mankind. It far exceeds what could conceivably be used to any good purpose, even in defense. It presents, I repeat, by the very fact of its existence, a danger greater than anything involved in the worst political possibilities of East-West relations. Our first task is to bring this situation under control. And this task begins with a restructuring of our own thinking.

2. THE SALT TALKS

As these words are being written, the SALT talks are about to reopen. This is good, so far as it goes. There cannot be too much in the way of communication between the two governments about the problems involved.

But even the best results that could be expected from these talks are unlikely to be enough. The main reason for this is that the pace of advancement in military technology is faster than the predictable pace of any negotiations of this nature. The technological background against which the instructions to the two delegations would be drawn up would be one that no longer entirely prevailed at the time they were concluded, so that any agreements reached would be bound to be partially overtaken by events.

But there is another and even more serious danger. Talks of this nature have in the past developed, and must almost inevitably develop, into contests to see how much one could contrive to keep, in the way of nuclear weaponry, and how much the other side could be brought to give up, as though the entire purpose of the exercise was simply to get the other party at a maximum disadvantage. This is probably inevitable, given the usual positions and the responsibilities of the negotiators on both sides. But it constitutes, in essence, only another reflection of the assumption of the ultimate supremacy of military values in the bilateral relationship — the very assumption, that is, which lies at the heart of the danger. So long as the view prevails that that party has won, in the SALT talks, which has contrived to retain a maximum of its own strategic nuclear power and has compelled the other party to give up a bit more of its own, I cannot see much progress being made in the reduction of nuclear armaments.

This is another way of saying that there is not much likelihood that adequate progress will be made in the SALT talks (adequate, that is, in relation to the depth and seriousness of the problem) unless those talks are accompanied by at least *some* measures of unilateral restraint in weapons developments on the part of both parties. This should not really be too difficult. The amount of nuclear destructive power now in American arsenals is said by the experts to be just about ten times what was originally calculated to be enough to make no war worthwhile from the Soviet standpoint. There is simply no need for all this overkill. Both sides could afford to give up four fifths of it tomorrow, and would still retain enough to serve all useful purposes. A unilateral reduction of 10 percent, immediately and as an act of good faith, could hurt neither of them.

But there are other fields, too, not directly related to the SALT talks, in which the United States could well afford to change its own position in the interests of a safer and more hopeful situation with respect to nuclear weaponry; and to these I must now turn.

3. NUCLEAR TESTING

There is no reason at all why the United States should not offer, on the basis of reciprocity from the Russian side, to give up all testing of nuclear explosives, of any sort. Not only would this not seriously jeopardize our defense but it would put us in a far better position to take the lead in attempting to induce the members of the rapidly growing company of states having a nuclear capability to do likewise.

I recognize that there are a number of people in our military and scientific establishments who are deeply committed to the underground testing of these explosives, and that scientific curiosity has some part in their commitment. But surely, the main purpose of these tests, as now pursued, is to find some gimmick that will suddenly give us an edge over the Russians in the designing and production of the weapons which employ the explosives in question. And this is exactly the kind of thinking that is going to have to stop, if this mad proliferation of nuclear destructive power is ever to be halted and reversed. If the Russians are willing to stop this testing, we should be prepared to do likewise. What is needed at this point is not to find more ingenious ways of detonating these devices but to learn how we can forestall and prevent their detonation in ways that cause devastation to thousands and millions of people.

4. The Principle of "First Use"

I have recounted, in my own memoirs, how, many years ago, in a memo addressed to the Secretary of State, I urged

that before we decide to proceed with the development of the hydrogen bomb, thus committing ourselves and the world to an indefinite escalation of the destructiveness and expensiveness of atomic weapons, we reexamine once more, in the most serious and solemn way, the whole principle of "first use" of atomic weapons or any other of the weapons of mass destruction; and I made it as clear as any language at my command could make it that if such a reexamination took place, my voice would be cast most decisively in favor of the abandonment of this principle altogether.

Today, twenty-seven years later, although the commitment to first use is now far more deeply imbedded in the theory and practice of ourselves and our allies than it was then, I see no reason to go back on this judgment. On the contrary, I am more convinced than ever that this pernicious theory has lain at the heart not only of the nuclear weapons race with the Soviet Union that has brought us all to such a parlous pass but also of the proliferation of nuclear weapons across the globe which we are now beginning to witness.

Our concern should be, of course, to achieve the eventual elimination of the nuclear weapon and all other weapons of mass destruction from national arsenals at the earliest possible moment. But it is clear that this will never be done so long as we ourselves are committed to the principle of first use — so long as we entertain, and encourage others in, the belief that never could we in the Western world assure our own defense except by initiating the use of these weapons or at least basing our defense plans on such initiation, which amounts to the same thing.

Only recently, the Soviet government proposed a general pact to assure that none of the signatories would be the first to resort to the use of weapons of this nature. This appeal was issued on the eve of a meeting of the NATO ministerial council. It was instantly rejected by that body without even so much as an internal discussion, let alone discussion with the Russians. So profound now is the commitment to the idea that never could NATO assure its own defense without resort to these weapons, and that their use would be justified to assure that defense, that the proposal was not considered worth examining.

I must question this reasoning. I see no reason why NATO could not, if it wanted, assure its own defense in an environment composed exclusively of conventional weapons. It might cost more; it might require a bit higher sacrifice from the respective peoples. Why not? Is the minor convenience that might be derived from escaping these burdens sufficient to overbalance a danger to all the populations of the northern hemisphere, indeed to Western civilization itself, greater than any ever before known? Are the comforts of this particular generation so sacred, do they have such weight in the great span of Western civilization of which we are only a small and fleeting part, that the entire progress and survival of that civilization has to be jeopardized to assure them? What egotism!

I saw it argued somewhere in the public prints, the other day, that we must at once strengthen the NATO forces in Europe because as things now stand we might easily be forced to fall back, in the event of a Russian attack, and then our tactical nuclear weapons, having a limited range, might fall on NATO territory already in the hands of the enemy, thus jeopardizing its NATO inhabitants, instead of the populations farther east. How shameful — this thought! As though the people farther east, who might otherwise have been struck by those weapons, were not people — as though it was somehow better and more tolerable for them, women, children and all, to be burned up than for people who were citizens of a NATO country — as if those Eastern Europeans, ostensibly the objects of our political sympathy, suffered less, or were of such inferiority that their sufferings mattered less in God's sight — and in ours. Was there ever a better example of the corruption worked on people's minds and assumptions by this habit of thinking about war in terms of nuclear weaponry — this concept of holding populations hostage with a view to extorting advantage from their governments?

This, and much more, is involved in the principle of first use. We cannot get away from it: either we approve of mass destruction as a means of warfare regardless of the disasters it holds for much of humanity, our own civilization included, and in implementation of this approval we cling to the principle of first use of these weapons, whether or not they are used against us; or we disapprove of it, in which case we should have the manliness to take the consequences of our feelings and to resolve that we shall not be the first to inaugurate this means of warfare — that we will find other means to assure our defense.

It is clear that we could not now get away from the principle of first use without consulting our NATO allies and making our best effort to persuade them of the necessity of what we are doing. They, even more hopelessly than ourselves (and, unfortunately, with our encouragement), have locked themselves into the belief that they could not possibly defend themselves without resorting to a form of weaponry that would make any real defense a mockery. Well, if so — so be it. The process of disabusing them of the false lessons we have taught them will of course take time. But has the moment not come to make a beginning?

Bear in mind that what is being suggested at this point is not that we should forgo all manufacture of nuclear weapons or all holding of them in our arsenals (though this, too, I should like to see happen) but only that we should not inaugurate the use of them — be the first to use them — in any military encounter. And there is no reason, in the light of the recent Soviet proposal for a pact to this effect, why this renunciation would have to be a unilateral one. The Soviet government has already offered, after all, to join us in such a step.

5. CONVENTIONAL WEAPONS

The above observations all run, obviously, to the forfeiture of such advantages as we conceive ourselves to enjoy through the cultivation of nuclear weaponry and the commitment to its first use in any serious military encounter. The first objection to this will be that this would leave us hopelessly outclassed in conventional weaponry, and unable, in particular, to defend Western Europe against a Russian attack.

To this, I can only say the following: If a strengthening of our posture in conventional weaponry is really needed, or to the extent it is needed, to assure our ability to meet our commitments to Western Europe and Japan, then that is that, and the added strength should be made available. But there are several reservations.

First, one would like to make sure that the estimates of Russian strength against which NATO's needs are calculated are plausible and realistic and do not contain the sort of exaggeration we have had occasion to note on many past occasions.

Secondly, one would like to be sure that the maximum effort has been made, in the Mutual and Balanced Force Reduction talks and elsewhere, to achieve a general reduction of the Warsaw Pact deployments in Eastern and Central Europe as well as the NATO ones. If any success is to be had along this line, it will probably be necessary at some point to reinforce the more or less public MBFR talks with more private, wide-ranging, and flexible ones.

Thirdly, one would like to be assured that our own military leaders are prepared to make the most of the equipment now available to them instead of designating it as obsolescent and relegating it to the junk piles or selling it to someone else in order to justify demands for fancier, more recent, and more sophisticated items.

Fourthly, one would like to feel the maximum improvement has been made in the fighting capacity of our conventional forces, ground, air and naval, by readjustments in their composition and their deployment. There have been a number of statements emanating from senior and highly experienced military figures to the effect that existing compositions and deployments are not fully suitable: that neither the positioning nor the equipment of certain NATO divisions, for example, is the best they might be; that the U.S. Navy should have less aircraft carriers on station abroad and a greater capacity for seaborne support of American forces overseas, and so on. The layman cannot judge the seriousness of these needs and possibilities. He can only note that the criticisms come from highly qualified people; and he would like to be sure that all possibilities for improvement along these lines have been explored and exhausted before the final bill for strengthening of conventional forces is presented.

Once these requirements have been satisfied, then I can see no objection to whatever strengthening of the conventional forces may be found necessary, provided the determination of necessity is an honest and realistic one. And if this really means that the defense budget cannot be appreciably reduced, so be it.

But then it is also important that this need for strengthening not be argued before Congress and public opinion on the basis of alarmist distortions of the pattern of Soviet intentions and the likelihood of hostile Soviet action. If a proper American defense posture can be had only by the use of such distortions, then it is better, for the moment, not to have it; for such misrepresentations invariably revenge themselves at a later date in the abuse they work on public opinion. Above all, the needs of national defense must not be presented to the American public in such a way as to suggest that a military outcome of our differences with the Russians is the most likely one, and military considerations are overriding in Soviet-American relations. If an adequate NATO defense establishment can be created in Europe only at the cost of persuading people that an armed conflict is ultimately inevitable or that the best we can hope for in East-West relations is a military standoff of indefinite duration based on an atmosphere of total suspicion and hostility, then I am not sure that the effort to achieve such an establishment would not be self-defeating; for no real security is to be attained along that line.

6. INTELLIGENCE

In the pattern of Soviet-American military rivalry and mutual suspicion, no one will ever know exactly what part has been played by the activities of the secret intelligence services on both sides; but that this part is a very large one is beyond question. I myself have had occasion to see instance after instance in which American intelligence authorities have mounted, or have attempted to mount, operations which have constituted, or would have constituted, a direct abuse not just of Soviet-American diplomatic relations in the formal sense but of the very possibilities for reaching a better understanding between the two governments. And I see no reason to suppose that the Soviet intelligence authorities have lagged in any way behind our own in this respect. A good example of the damage these activities can do will be found in the effect of the U-2 episode, in 1960, on the summit meeting then under contemplation.

One of the most dangerous aspects of these far-flung and extravagant efforts at snooping is that they, like many of the regular military preparations, reflect a pattern of assumptions in which the relationship between the two countries in question is virtually indistinguishable from what would prevail if a state of war already existed or if the early coming-into-existence of such a state of war was regarded as inevitable. But such assumptions, once made the basis for governmental activity on an extensive scale, soon come to take on reality in the minds of those who are called upon to act on the basis of them; and they then have a contagious effect — both on the remainder of the governmental establishment within which they operate and also on the one against which they are directed.

A second and no smaller element of danger, inherent in these activities, is the great difficulty of controlling and adjusting them to the needs of a constructive relationship. Their very nature requires that they be known to very few people. Thus many of those in high position who might have the authority and the wisdom to control them cannot do so because they know nothing about them. But beyond this, even where they are known, it is a bold and risky thing for a civilian official, such as a career ambassador, to try to place, or even to recommend, restrictions on them, for he can easily thereby put himself in the position of one who obstructs efforts and operations regarded as necessary to the national defense.

Activities of this nature do not normally enter into the exchanges and discussions between governments, although the discussants often have those of the other party prominently in mind, as causes for suspicion, even as they talk of other things. This, in fact, is a further aspect of the danger that surrounds them. In 1972, to be sure, the great risks of accident then being presented by the mutual shadowing of Soviet and American naval vessels at sea were made the subject of discussion between the two governments, and an agreement was arrived at, useful but very limited in scope, to reduce the danger of collisions. This was, however, a beginning that scarcely scratched the surface of the larger problem to which it related.

It might be thought that a general betterment of the atmosphere of Soviet-American relations would find reflection in a diminution in the intensity and dangerousness of efforts of this nature. Unfortunately, one must expect that if such an improvement were to occur, the operatives of secret military intelligence would be the last to take note of it and to be influenced by it, unless they were to receive specific instructions from their superiors to place limits on their activities.

If the trend towards militarization of the Soviet-American relationship is to be abated and reversed, I see nothing for it but that the governments must take acount of this problem, must do what they can unilaterally to temper the recklessness and dangerousness of much of what is now occurring in this field, and must then, at the suitable time and in the suitable forum, find means to consult together with a view to finding further means to curb and control activities of this nature. If war is not really inevitable or even probable, then our lives do not depend primarily on how much we can learn that someone else does not want us to know about his doings, and how much we can conceal about our own.

A total abandonment of secret intelligence gathering (as distinct from secret political operations, which constitute another subject) is not to be expected. It was a normal feature of the policies of national states long before either the Soviet Union or even the United States came into existence; and it would be utopian to hope for its total disappearance. But there are limits. It is one of those instances where, as Shakespeare observed: "Take but degree away, and hark what discord follows." The problem is not to abolish secret intelligence. The problem is to see that it does not get out of hand, which it has been — both on their part and on ours — in a fair way of doing.

7. THE DISSIDENTS AND HUMAN RIGHTS

In the late 1880s a cousin of my grandfather, bearing the same name as myself, wrote, after a long and arduous journey of investigation in Siberia, a book entitled *Siberia and the Exile System* in which he described the sufferings of the political prisoners and exiles who had been sent to that region by the Tsarist authorities by way of punishment for their various efforts of opposition — some not very violent, some extremely so — against the Tsarist regime. The book was something of a sensation, was translated into many languages (there was even an illegal Russian edition), made a deep impression everywhere, and had a lasting effect, in particular, on the attitudes of the educated Western public of that day towards Tsarist Russia. This effect could still be felt, in fact, at the time of the Russian Revolution, in the enthusiasm with which large parts of the Western public welcomed that event.

Twenty years after the Revolution, Russian society, and particularly intellectual society, fell victim at the hands of Stalin and his henchmen to a regime of terror second to nothing ever experienced by any great country in the modern age — a regime many times worse in scale and brutality than anything which the elder George Kennan had ever been obliged to observe. A whole generation of writers, artists, actors, directors, intelligentsia of all sorts, many of them talented people, were swept away, together with millions of other people, in this vast holocaust. Strangely enough, however, while the relatively mild Tsarist acts of oppression had produced torrents of protest in Western countries, these terrible purges of the period 1935 to 1939 did not, nor did the equally horrible measures taken during World War II against certain minority peoples of the USSR, and against the populations of certain of the areas overrun by Soviet forces. The victims of *these* persecutions, including such great figures as the poet Mandelstam, went, so far as the Western world was concerned, silently, obscurely, and helplessly to their martyrdom and death.

Forty years have elapsed since that terrible time. The regime now in power in Russia takes measures, too, against those of its citizens who oppose it, who publicly disagree with it, or who make trouble for it in other ways. These measures, like those of the Tsar's government nearly a century ago, are often stupid, unfeeling, needlessly brutal, bound to aggravate the very contumacy against which they are directed. In scale and severity, however, they are incomparably smaller and less horrible than those undertaken by the Stalinist police system in the 1930s. The present dissidents, unhappy as is their situation, are treated — relatively speaking — with a liberality which in Stalin's day would have been unthinkable: permitted to reside, in many instances, in their homes in Moscow, to write their dissenting literature and to distribute it privately, to consort with foreigners, to take their complaints to foreign correspondents and to appeal through them to the sympathies of the outside world.

I would not like to be misunderstood. I am far from approving of the treatment these people are receiving at the hands of the Soviet police. I feel almost sorry for a regime whose sense of weakness is so great that it cannot find better ways than this to cope with differences of opinion between itself and a relatively small and helpless band of intellectuals. But honesty compels me to note — and I think my readers should note — that compared with what existed forty years ago, what we have before us today, unjust and uncalled for as it may appear in our eyes, is progress. And yet it is the object of Western press attention and Western protests on a scale far more extensive than were the much greater excesses of the Stalin period. The new American administration even finds itself faced with demands, from both outside and inside its own ranks, that it should go much further and should make the treatment of the dissidents the decisive touchstone of Soviet-American relations, if necessary to the detriment of progress in other areas of the relationship.

What conclusions, one wonders, are the Soviet leaders to draw from this state of affairs? Are they expected to conclude that although greater mildness in the treatment of dissidence, in comparison with the Stalin period, has now led to a marked increase in foreign indignation and protest, further mildness will have the opposite effect, causing oppositionist activities in Russia to subside and taking the heat off the Western reaction? Or are they going to conclude that Stalin was essentially right after all — that the only way to maintain a firm Communist dictatorship and to make the Western world accept it is to punish dissidence as Stalin did: with such prompt and fearful terror that the Western press never even hears about the sufferings and fate of the victims? Are they going to conclude, finally, that they were wrong to relax as much as they *have* relaxed, that a mile will be taken wherever an inch is given, and that to yield further would be to embark on a path that would lead eventually to the destruction of the regime itself?

In this, Western policy-makers have the heart of the dilemma; for while a little pressure from Western opinion may be useful, too much of it can cause the Kremlin to feel that what is at stake for it is self-preservation; and then there will be no question of yielding, for self-preservation is a consideration that would take precedence over any other considerations, all the rest of Soviet-American relations included; and where there is no question of yielding, there will be no benefit brought to those on whose behalf these protests are being made — only harm to U.S.-Soviet relations.

The Soviet government asked for trouble, of course, when it signed the Helsinki declarations on human rights. The Western governments are formally on good ground in making this an issue of their relations with Moscow, if they care to do so. But the question remains as to whether it is wise for them to proceed much farther along this path: whether this will significantly benefit the people on whose behalf they are being asked to intervene; and, if so, whether this benefit will be of such importance as to outweigh the progress that might, in other circumstances, be made in other fields.

I should perhaps explain that I yield to no one in my admiration for such men as Solzhenitsyn and Sakharov; I would place them among the greatest Russians of the modern age. Were I a Russian, they would have my deepest gratitude and, I suppose (it is always dangerous to think you know how noble you would be in hypothetical circumstances), my support.

But I am not a Russian. Neither are all those for whom the U.S. government professes to be the spokesman. I have tried, in this book, to place myself in the position of the U.S. government, to look at things from the standpoint of its responsibilities, and to establish something resembling priorities between these various responsibilities where they conflict.

Among those responsibilities, the task of overthrowing the Soviet government, or bringing about a fundamental change in its nature, does not, as I see it, figure. There are limits to what we can put upon ourselves. It is enough for us to find our own way out of the labyrinth of problems in which the modern age is enveloping us and to create conditions within our own country with which we can profess ourselves satisfied. With relation to the Soviet government, our task is not to destroy it or make it into something else but to find means of living side by side with it and dealing with it which serve to diminish rather than to increase the dangers that now confront us all.

General George Marshall used to say to those who worked for him: Don't fight the problem. I have been going here, and I think the U.S. government must go, on the theory that the problem, in this case, is the Soviet government as it is, as we find it, and as it is probably going to continue to be for some time into the future. I have never advocated an American policy aimed at its overthrow — have in fact actively opposed such a policy — not because the form of government prevailing in Russia commends itself to my tastes and sympathies but because I do not think it our business to try to determine political developments in other countries, because we would probably not be able to do this even if we wanted to, and because we would not know what to put in the place of the present Russian regime even if we succeeded in overthrowing it. I know of no potential democratic Russian governments standing in the wings.

Now, we may not see an American governmental policy which includes support for the Soviet dissidents as one aimed at the overthrow of Soviet power. Not all of the dissidents see their own activity that way. It may be argued that what is involved here is not an effort to overthrow that power or to change its fundamental nature but rather to make plain the strength of American sympathy for those who suffer from its excesses, and the warmth of the American desire to see its practices conform more closely to the universal ideals of tolerance and respect for what have now come to be known as human rights.

To this, on principle, no objection can be raised. The American sympathies in question really exist. There is the Soviet signature beneath the Helsinki declarations. There can be no objection, surely, to the expression by responsible American officials of their hope, and the hope of those they represent, that these undertakings will someday find recognition not just in the words but also in the policies and practices of the Soviet government.

I will go even further. It would not be unreasonable for the U.S. government to make it clear to its Soviet counterpart that so long as there continue to exist the conditions of which we are being daily reminded by the foreign press corps in Moscow — so long, in other words, as the Soviet police authorities continue to over-react and to proceed stupidly, unfeelingly and with brutality against men and women whose only offense has been to voice, in restrained and unprovocative fashion, views divergent from those to which the regime is, and has been for sixty years, committed — so long as things are this way there will be, and must be, limits beyond which Soviet-American relations cannot develop — limits to the extent to which Americans, either in their personal capacity or through their government, could ever associate themselves with Soviet purposes and ideals, as revealed in present Soviet practice. So long, in other words, as these conditions persist, there must always be maintained a certain distance between the two governments — a distance which no summit meetings, no warm toasts, no friendship societies, no cultural cooperation, and no talk of coexistence can overcome — a distance which, considering the immense responsibilities that rest on both governments from the standpoint of preserving world peace and designing a safer and better world, can only be called tragic. This is the way things will have to be; and for this the Soviet authorities must hold only themselves to blame.

On the other hand, what is most important about many things that are done in international life, as elsewhere, is not *whether* they are done but *how*. There are ways and ways of making plain to the Soviet leaders and to the world how America reacts to the reports of the treatment of the dissidents. Some criticisms are useful; some destructive. Pressures to a given point may yield results; pressures beyond that point may be self-defeating.

The task of the U.S. government will be to see how these feelings of the American people can be communicated to the Soviet government in a way that will help, rather than damage, the fortunes of those to whose strivings and sufferings they are addressed. But this government will also have to be concerned to see that these expressions of sympathy do not take forms that are misinterpreted in Moscow as direct efforts to shape the course of internal political developments in Russia, and that they do not, in this way, interfere with the completion of the main task of American statesmanship with relation to Russia, which is, as noted above, to reduce the danger posed for both countries and for the world by the present military rivalry.

8. TRADE

The Soviet government has always attached, and continues to attach, great importance to the possibilities for the development of Soviet-American trade. The reasons for this are no doubt various. They include such practical considerations as a desire to tap America's rich resources of advanced technology, the need for heavy importations of American grain to make up domestic agricultural deficiencies, and so on. But there has also always been a curious feeling on the part of Soviet leaders that a willingness to expand trade, or at least to make public gestures in that direction, is a symbol of a desire to strengthen political relations, particularly in the case of a capitalist country, and therefore has high political significance.

It is difficult for the United States government to respond to such a view. It does not control trade, and cannot, for the most part, increase or decrease it. The trade has to flow, for better or for worse, from whatever commercial incentive can be given to private traders.

Despite the obvious asymmetries between a state trading system, on the one hand, and a system of private trading initiative such as we have, on the other, there is no reason why we should wish to discourage trade with the Soviet Union, provided only that it does not lead to so high a degree of dependence of individual American firms, or groups of firms, on Soviet orders that it would give to the Soviet trade monopoly an undue influence in our affairs, as our oil dependence has given to the Arabs and others, and provided the Soviet Union is not permitted to acquire, through normal trading transactions, access to sophisticated American technology which would have military value and which we would not normally, as a matter of governmental policy, have made available to it. Of this last, our government has to be the judge; and it should see that such transfers of technology do not occur. But here, one should be very sure: first, that the technology in question really is of high and sensitive military value, and could not be produced in the Soviet Union; and secondly, that the Russians could not obtain it from other sources. It will be found, I believe, that the area of technology that could meet both of these criteria is very narrow indeed.

Beyond these rather elementary precautions there is, I repeat, no reason to discourage Soviet-American trade. The idea that trade promotes useful human contacts and conduces to good will and peace can easily be carried too far, particularly when it concerns trade with a foreign governmental trade monopoly. But if it does not do a great deal of good, psychologically and from the standpoint of human contacts, it also does not do any great harm; on the contrary, it is probably mildly useful in convincing people on both sides that their opposite numbers are human beings, not monsters, and that we all live in the same world. In addition to which there is the often forgotten fact that it is economically useful.

In these circumstances, I can see no reason whatsoever why most-favored-nation treatment should be withheld in the case of the Soviet Union. The withholding of it as a device for putting pressure on the Soviet government in the question of Jewish emigration has been obviously unsuccessful — so much so that the case for its abandonment need no longer be seriously argued. And other justifications for this practice are not apparent. The trade has been massively in our favor in recent years; so protectionist considerations are scarcely relevant.

There have been suggestions that we should withhold m.f.n. treatment, and indeed discourage trade itself, as a means of extorting political concessions generally — that we should not permit grain exports to proceed, for example, unless the Soviet Union consents to give us concessions in other, and unrelated, fields. This idea seems to me to be quite unsound; it is in any case impracticable. When the Soviet trade monopoly enters the American market as a buyer, it pays, or should pay, the going price — the market price, that is — for whatever it buys. If the American seller does not demand more, and consents to sell at that price, and the Soviet trade monopoly then pays it, it has a right to assume that it has done all that could reasonably be asked of it as a trader, and has a right to take possession of the goods for which it paid. We cannot then logically come along afterwards, as a government, and say in effect: "You must pay for this all over again in the form of this or that political price, before you can have the goods." Either we believe in free enterprise and the validity of the market or we do not. If we do, we should concede that to pay the going price is payment enough. If we do not, then we should establish a governmental trade monopoly ourselves and conduct trade for political reasons.

The view that trade with Communist countries (because this affects not Soviet Russia alone) should be used as an instrument for extorting political concessions implies, first, that we do not really need the trade for economic-financial reasons—that we, as a country, derive no significant commercial profit from it and can easily take it or leave it; and, secondly, that for us to consent to trade with another country represents some sort of an act of grace on our part, for which the other party should be willing to pay both the usual commercial price and a political premium as well. Neither of these implications will stand in the case of our trade with the Soviet Union: the first will not because the balance in our favor, averaging several hundred million dollars a year in recent years, is by no means a negligible factor in the calculations of a country which has a balance of payments problem; and the second, because it will simply not be accepted there or anywhere.

We may as well accommodate ourselves, therefore, to letting Americans trade with the Soviet Union wherever they find it profitable to do so, conceding m.f.n. treatment to the Soviet exports to this country, and merely keeping a watchful eye open to assure that sensitive military technology is not unintentionally revealed in this way and that undue relationships of dependence on the Soviet trade monopoly do not develop. The resulting involvements will constitute a certain small anchor to windward in the tenser moments, and we should both profit from the exchanges.

I see, on the other hand, no reason why we should extend extensive government credits beyond those that would fit the pattern of the normal operations of the Export-Import Bank. The Soviet Union has formidable financial resources of its own — sufficient to enable it to conduct in various parts of the world political operations, including massive arms shipments, which we find unhelpful to world political stability. I can see no reason why we should assist it along this line. To which must be added the reflection that the Soviet authorities have never been very forthcoming about their own financial situation. Something in my own Scottish ancestry rebels, I am afraid, against the suggestion that you should lend large amounts of money to someone else whose actual financial situation is assiduously concealed from you.

9. Cultural Relations

At the height of the Nixon-Kissinger détente — in the period 1972–1974 — a number of bilateral intergovernmental agreements were concluded between the Soviet government and U.S. government for cooperation in various fields of science, technology, and public health. In addition to these, there are agreements between private institutions in the United States and various Soviet institutions, involving exchanges of one sort or another.

In the many criticisms that have recently been levied against détente, these agreements and their consequences have been generally forgotten; one gains the impression, in fact, that most of the critics have never heard of them, or consider them insignificant.

Actually, the results of these agreements are not insignificant, nor are they, on balance, negative. Certain of the contemplated exchanges and other forms of cooperation have run into initial difficulties, usually due to unfamiliarity of the Soviet side with cooperative efforts of this nature — sometimes to bureaucratic hesitations and timidities of one sort or another. In addition, certain agreements in the commercial field have remained unimplemented as a consequence of the failure of the commercial agreement of 1972 to gain congressional ratification in Washington. But by and large, the Soviet authorities seem to have tried, in good faith, to carry out their end of these arrangements. Some, especially the agreements in the field of public health and the various arrangements for academic exchange, have proved strongly beneficial. Two hundred scientists (one hundred from each side) are collaborating, for example, on medical research; and Dr. Theodore Cooper, Assistant Secretary for Health, Education and Welfare, has expressed publicly the view that American research in this field gained importantly from the experience. All in all, there is no reason to doubt that as initial hesitations are overcome and familiarity grows with the attendant procedures, significant results will be achieved for both sides.

Certain of the agreements are criticized from the American military and hard-line side, on the grounds that the Russians get more information about us out of them than we get about them. This charge obviously reflects a view analogous to that referred to above in connection with negotiations on the control of armaments: namely, that their gain can only be our loss and vice versa — that the purpose of the American side in these agreements is to see how much information it can gain from the Soviet side and how little it can contrive to give up in exchange.

Of this it can only be said that if this — the gathering of military or quasi-military intelligence — was really the purpose our people had in mind in concluding these agreements, it would have been better not to conclude them in the first place. But I see no reason to suppose that it was. The greatest benefit we derive from these arrangements lies in the field of the intangibles: the greater mutual acquaintance between experts on both sides of the line — the breakdown of unreal stereotypes in the minds of both parties — the discovery that not all those on the other side are inhuman and that we actually have a good deal in common. The effect of the agreements in this respect should not be underrated. The number of experts exchanging visits in this way has risen by at least 300 percent since the agreements were pursued, and is now running at two to three thousand per annum in both directions. The positive results of such exposure to the people and surroundings of the other country are of course not immediately visible, and cannot be measured just in terms of the information derived by our side. But the information the Russians obtain from us by this means is, as a rule, information they could obtain from other sources if they wanted to; whereas these intangible benefits which we particularly value are ones it would be difficult to produce in any other way.

Beyond this, it takes a rather smug and provincial view of this relationship to assume that we have nothing to learn from professional contacts of this nature other than such technical information as we can eke out of our opposite numbers. We are human beings ourselves, supposedly, as are they; and who is to say that we could not enrich our own way of looking at things by a thoughtful and serious attention to theirs? The fact that their system may not appeal to us is no reason why their experiences and reactions, as human beings, could not be informative, and could not shed some light on our problems.

Naturally, cultural relations, like other ones, must be a two-way street if they are to be fruitful; and if there were reason to believe that the Russians were viewing them from a standpoint of total cynicism and surrounding them with such restrictions and conditions that the direct benefits, from the substantive side, were negligible, and the intangible ones nonexistent, I would be the first to urge their termination. I see no evidence of such an attitude in what I can learn of the operation of the agreements now in force. And until such evidence is forthcoming, it seems to me that this, one of the few potentially constructive aspects of the relationship, should not be forgotten, ignored, or lightly sacrificed to totally unconstructive undertakings.

10. PROFESSIONALISM AND THE MOSCOW EMBASSY

Effective diplomacy is not just a matter of grand strategy. It is also a matter of the information and advice one seeks, the people one uses, and the channels for communication one selects for the implementation of policy. In all these respects the practices of the U.S. government in recent years, in relations with the Soviet Union, have left a good deal to be desired.

There can be no question but that the American political establishment has a long-standing, almost traditional aversion to professionalism in diplomacy. The principle on which it proceeds is that experience in any other conceivable walk of professional life — the law, business, journalism, you name it — would obviously be a better qualification for senior responsibility in the diplomatic field than experience in the Foreign Service itself.

It is not my purpose here to polemize against this concept in its wider application. But it strikes me as being particularly question-able when applied to our relations with Russia; and I believe that our government, by adhering to it, is depriving itself of some of the most valuable resources that lie at its disposal.

If I am not mistaken, there has not been a time since the termina-tion of the ambassadorship of the late Llewellyn Thompson when the American embassy in Moscow has been used to any significant extent either as a source of information and day-by-day advice for high-level policy-making, or as a channel for the presentation of Washington's point of view and the explanation of its policies to the appropriate levels of officialdom in Moscow. On one occasion our ambassador was excluded not only from personal participation in ne-gotiations highly relevant to his official responsibilities but even from access to adequate information about what was going on. There seems to have been a belief in Washington that information about Russia could better come through other channels than the regular diplomatic ones; that those charged with the conduct of foreign pol-icy in Washington were in no particular need of professional advice, especially from the field; and that the task of explaining Washing-ton's position to people in Moscow could safely be left to occasional visits by high-ranking American figures to Moscow, to chance en-counters by those figures with their Soviet opposite numbers at in-ternational gatherings, or to discussions with the Soviet ambassador in Washington. Aside from all questions of personality, this view embraces some serious functional miscalculations.

By failing to use the American embassy, senior policy-makers in Washington are simply wasting the services in Moscow of the men who, of all those who are concerned with the problem of Soviet-American relations, are closest to the problem, live daily in constant exposure to the source of it, follow the situation from day to day, are sensitive to divergencies between the external rhetoric and internal reality in Soviet policy, and have a feel for all that is in-volved. Most of the officers of that diplomatic mission know some Russian and have had special training of one sort or another for their work — not as much training, to be sure, as they ought to have, because Washington does not give it to them, but more than the great majority of those whose voices are customarily heard in policy formulation. It is painful to see prominent and influential congressional figures sitting humbly at the feet of visiting Russian dissidents in the search for information about Russia, when people far more detached, better schooled in American interests, and better equipped by motivation to tell them what they ought to know never even meet a member of Congress. Some of these dissident figures are of course great men; but it is not the interests of the United States — sometimes not even those of world peace — that they have at heart; and much as they may know about internal conditions in Russia, they are often the merest children when it comes to the understanding of international relations.

By failing to use the Moscow embassy as a channel for informing Soviet officialdom of Washington's views one deprives that mission of much of its potential value as a source of information on Soviet outlooks and policies; for no more in diplomacy than in any other walk of life is something normally given for nothing; and Soviet officials are not going to be greatly interested in discussing American policy with American representatives in Moscow who are themselves very poorly informed with regard to it.

But beyond this, the task of making Washington's views known in Moscow and gaining understanding for them on the part of Soviet officialdom is not one that can be adequately performed by sporadic encounters between various personalities at the most senior levels. Not only are the senior American figures concerned not always cognizant of the real meaning and background for the words and expressions used by their Soviet opposite numbers, even when faithfully translated, but there is also the fact that Washington's point of view, if it is to be effectively presented, has to be put currently, almost daily, to people in the official Soviet establishment, has to be put by persons who know how to put it, linguistically and otherwise, and has to be put not just at one level but a variety of them — something which the embassy, with its wide set of contacts, is uniquely capable of doing.

A wise American diplomacy with relation to the Soviet Union will be concerned to improve the professional resources it has to help it with this problem, and will then see to it that such resources as it has are used, not neglected.

XIV

A Global Concept
of American Policy

EVERY AMERICAN ADMINISTRATION OF RECENT YEARS HAS BEEN RE-
peatedly charged with having no grand design for foreign policy —
no general concept into which the various regional and functional
undertakings would fit in some coherent and mutually consistent
way. It is my hope that the considerations set forth above, little apt
as some of them are to command general and instantaneous agreement, will at least constitute a concept which would answer to that
description. And I shall now attempt to describe, by way of sum-
mary, what the concept in question would look like.

One would begin with a realistic recognition of the many limitations that rest upon the United States government — some constitu-
tional, some ones of tradition and patterns of thought, some ones of
the workings of the political system, some the reflections of situations into which we have worked ourselves — from the standpoint
of the conduct of foreign policy. Wherever possible, of course, we
would act to remove or to alleviate these limitations; and we would
begin, promptly and resolutely, with the most serious of them: the
undue dependence on foreign oil, and particularly on oil that is in
potentially unreliable foreign hands.

Recognizing, however, that most of the remaining limitations are

[228]

ones we could not, for domestic-political reasons, remove, we would take the consequences of this relative helplessness and accept the fact that there are severe limits on what we may expect to accomplish in the way of influencing the course of world events — that we will be lucky enough if we succeed in protecting the security of our own people as well as of those few foreign peoples who are reasonably aware of their own stake in the endurance and prospering of American society as we know it and whose friendship is essential to our security. We would, in other words, approach the problems of foreign policy with a relative humility, bearing in mind that our resources are finite and that we are faced with certain urgent and difficult but limited tasks, the successful accomplishment of which is essential to world security and to our own; that we must concentrate on the performance of these tasks if we are to have any chance of completing them; that we cannot, for this reason, afford to dissipate our attention, our energies, and our resources on those dreams of world betterment, that pursuit of global involvement and authority, and that moralistic posturing, which are so congenial to the American political temperament and to the rhetoric of our public life.

This means, of course, the reduction of external commitments to the indispensable minimum. And I would see this minimum in the preservation of the political independence and military security of Western Europe, of Japan, and — with the single reservation that it should not involve the dispatch and commitment of American armed forces — of Israel. These commitments would constitute the hard core of our external obligations, and they would be given all necessary priority. To the extent that the meeting of these obligations really demanded changes, improvements, and the strengthening of our armed forces and those of our allies, all that would be done. But it would be done, and so explained to our own and world opinion, as a response to the dictates of normal prudence; we would not conjure up fictitious threats from the Soviet or any other side merely for the purpose of drumming up public and legislative support for the measures in question.

In order to concentrate our resources and efforts on these essential tasks, we would, as noted above, ruthlessly eliminate ulterior commitments and involvements that would distract us from their performance. This would involve the abandonment of several obsolescent and nonessential positions: notably those at Panama, in the Philippines, and in Korea. It would involve the restoration to our Western European allies, who are the proper bearers of it, of the responsibility for shaping the future relationship of Greece and Turkey to NATO and for working out with the governments of those two countries the disposition of NATO military facilities and garrisons on their territory. American facilities and garrisons would no longer be maintained there.

In the case of Southern Africa we would take cognizance of the tragic profundity of the conflicts with which that region is racked, and of the inability of ourselves or any other outside party to suggest or invent happy solutions to those problems. We would not, then, take sides, but would confine our efforts to whatever we could do in the way of moderating passions and reducing violence. We would not, in particular, allow ourselves to be maneuvered into any form of involvement — either by the whites, who would like to frighten us into supporting them by depicting their opponents as the representatives of world communism, or by the black Africans, who would like to frighten us with the specter of the loss of the love (a highly questionable commodity in any case) of the remainder of black Africa.

As for the rest of the Third World, we would take account, again, of our general helplessness in the face of its problems — helplessness, first of all, because of the enormity of those problems in relation to our resources; helplessness again, because of the necessity of concentrating our resources and efforts elsewhere. We would not withdraw all interest in the affairs of that great part of the world nor would we deny it such developmental assistance as we could give through the international organizations. We would attempt to remove or reduce those aspects of our own protectionism that particularly affect the products of Third World countries. But beyond that we would not overly concern ourselves for words and reactions of the governments of this area, remembering that the best we can expect from them, over the long run, is their respect, not their liking or their gratitude.

In the Near East, we would moderate our enthusiasm for putting fantastic quantities of arms into the hands of peoples unable to make any proper use of them, and concentrate (always bearing in mind the commitment to Israel) on the task, first, of encouraging gradual accommodation between Israel and its Arab neighbors, and, secondly, on reaching such an understanding with the Soviet government as would assure against this region's becoming the source of serious conflict between the two great powers.

In the Far East, we would give primary attention to the shaping of our relationship with Japan, taking care to pay due heed to the real difficulties of communication with which that relationship is encumbered, and insisting that the conduct of relations, on a day-to-day basis, be in the hands of people specially prepared, linguistically, intellectually, and by experience, for that delicate and exacting function.

With relation to China, we would tread warily and not too fast, recognizing the great differences in the psychology of the two peoples as well as those that mark the ideals and purposes of the two governments; and we would try to keep ourselves as aloof as possible from involvement in the solution of the Taiwan problem. All this can and should be done without neglecting, or failing to manifest, the great respect Americans have traditionally had for Chinese civilization and the sympathy they have felt for the vicissitudes of Chinese life in this modern age.

As for Korea, we would extract ourselves, as gently and prudently as we can, from our military involvement in that country, taking particular care to keep close to the Japanese (whose interests are most sensitively involved) in all our words and actions.

Finally, with respect to the Soviet Union: we would address ourselves, first and foremost, to the urgent question of arms control, particularly in the area of strategic weaponry, endeavoring, the while, to enlighten and restrain those vociferous elements in our own society who have highly unreal ideas of the nature of Soviet power, who are temperamentally inclined to see the future of the relationship in purely military terms, and who would have us reach to new and even more fantastic heights in the production of nuclear weaponry and in the militarization of the relationship generally. We would recognize the need for unilateral measures of restraint. We would move to ease the process of arms control by consenting at once to a complete cessation of the testing of nuclear weapons. We would ourselves accept, and try to explain to our allies, the need for abandonment of the principle of first use and the conclusion of a suitable agreement on this subject with the Russians (as they have themselves proposed). We would see whether we could not get the cooperation of the Soviet government in restraining the more ebullient undertakings of the two intelligence services. We would not discourage trade; on the contrary we would welcome it and encourage it, among other things by the extension of most-favored-nation treatment; but we would not try to stimulate it by large-scale governmental credits, nor would we leave the Russians in any doubt that it would have to be the forces of the market, not governmental undertakings, that would determine its shape and dimensions.

With respect to the dissidents, we would not shrink from reminding the Soviet authorities of the negative feelings aroused among our people by the reports of the measures taken against these people by the Soviet police authorities. We would continue to make it clear that the continued pursuit by those authorities of practices so offensive to American opinion could not fail to constitute a burden on the relationship and to place limits on the extent to which it could be developed. But we would be careful not to give the Soviet leaders the impression that the United States government was exerting itself, in connivance with some of its own citizens, to encompass its overthrow, and we would avoid actions and gestures that smacked of direct interference in Soviet internal affairs.

We would, finally, improve our modalities for conducting the relationship at our end, placing less reliance on the arts of summitry and assigning a greater part of the burden to the less conspicuous but steadier and more effective labors of specially trained diplomatic professionals.

In this rapidly changing world, the complexity of the problems of which is beyond the powers of apprehension by any single mind or mathematical computer, it is idle to look too far ahead. The statesman can only ask what would be, in the immediate sense, most useful, and then apply himself, with such resources as he has at his command, to the accomplishment of it.

The purpose of the course outlined above would not be to move humanity into some new general level of altruism, peace, prosperity, and brotherhood. Recognizing that men are what they are and will not soon cease to be it, we would not expect that at the foreseeable end of these labors — say, in approximately three or four years' time (which is about the limit of the useful efforts at foresight by any statesman) — wars would have been abolished from the earth, human rights established everywhere, and peoples and governments everywhere brought to view the United States with gratitude, admiration, and love. What we would hope — and might even, I think, dare to expect — would be that at the end of this period the cloud of danger presented for all of us by the enormous cultivation and spread of nuclear weapons might be on its way to dissipation; that a more reassuring relationship might be in process of creation between Russia and the advanced West; and that men and governments, at least throughout the more highly developed northern hemisphere, would be breathing a bit more easily and would be prepared to turn from the fixations of military rivalry to more constructive and hopeful tasks — notably, the restoring of a healthy balance between modern industrial civilization and the natural environment in which it is rooted, and the discovery of a better relation — a relation that would give more spiritual sustenance and hope — of man to himself, and man to his fellow men, in an age of high technological achievement and material abundance.